Sir Douglas Galton

An Address on the General Principles Which Should be Observed in the Construction of Hospitals

Sir Douglas Galton

An Address on the General Principles Which Should be Observed in the Construction of Hospitals

ISBN/EAN: 9783337168247

Printed in Europe, USA, Canada, Australia, Japan

Cover: Foto ©ninafisch / pixelio.de

More available books at **www.hansebooks.com**

AN ADDRESS

ON THE GENERAL PRINCIPLES WHICH SHOULD BE OBSERVED IN THE

CONSTRUCTION OF HOSPITALS,

Delivered to the British Medical Association at Leeds,

JULY 29, 1869,

WITH THE DISCUSSION WHICH TOOK PLACE THEREON.

BY

DOUGLAS GALTON, C.B. F.R.S.

LATE A CAPTAIN ROYAL ENGINEERS,
HONORARY MEMBER OF THE BRITISH MEDICAL ASSOCIATION.

Printed by permission of the Council of the British Medical Association.

London:
MACMILLAN AND CO.
1869.

CONTENTS.

	PAGE
PREFACE	vii
ADDRESS	1
SITES OF HOSPITALS	3
Clear area on which a Hospital should stand	5
FORM AND DISTRIBUTION OF THE PARTS	5
Basis of Hospital Construction is the Ward	5
Conditions which regulate the Size of Wards	6
Conditions which regulate the Form of Wards	8
Maintenance of Purity in the Air	8
Superficial Area per bed	18
Way in which Space in a Ward should be laid out	20
Cubic Space resulting from these Conditions	21
Materials for, and other details of, Ward Construction	22
Ward Offices	28
Nurse's Room	28
Ward Scullery	29
Ablution Room, Water Closets, &c.	30
Drainage	33
Proportion of Ward Offices to Wards	34
Unit of Hospital Construction	35
AGGREGATION OF WARD UNITS IN THE CONSTRUCTION OF A HOSPITAL	35
ADMINISTRATIVE BUILDINGS	41
ECONOMICAL CONSIDERATIONS AFFECTING HOSPITAL CONSTRUCTION	44
APPLICATION OF PRINCIPLES TO EXISTING HOSPITALS	45
Cost of some existing Hospitals	54
CONCLUSION	55

DISCUSSION:—

	PAGE
Dr. Kennedy	57
Mr. Hutchinson	62
Sir James Simpson	65
Dr. Rumsey	70
Dr. Stewart	72
Dr. Hughes Bennett	73
Dr. Macleod	76

APPENDIX:—

Ventilating Fireplaces	81

LIST OF ILLUSTRATIONS.

FIG.		PAGE
1.	Plan of Ward and Ward Offices	35
2.	Plan of King's College Hospital, London	46
3.	Plan of Wards and Ward Offices at the Royal Victoria Hospital, Netley.	ib.
4.	Plan of Military Regimental Hospital	48
5.	General Plan of Swansea New Hospital	49
6.	General Plan of the Lariboisière Hospital, Paris	50
7.	General Plan of New Hospital at Leeds	51
8.	General Plan of Herbert Hospital, Woolwich	53
9.	Sketch of the Ends of the Southern Pavilions of the Herbert Hospital, showing the Elevation of the Central Corridor	54
10.	Elevation, showing Air and Smoke Flues	86
11.	Section of a Room showing Air-duct and Flue	ib.
12.	Section of Grate	ib.
13.	Plan of Grate and Air-chamber	ib.
14.	Fireplaces in Use at the Herbert Hospital	89
15.	Grate adopted by the War Department	91

PREFACE.

THE question of Hospital Construction embraces so wide a field that a detailed account of the subject would occupy far more time than a meeting like that of the British Medical Association at Leeds could afford. Each hospital, like each house, must be suited to the special wants and the special circumstances of the locality in which it is placed. To these the architect must adapt each design which he makes, but in the adaptation he must not depart from the fixed principles which should govern all designs.

I have in the following address, therefore, endeavoured to confine myself to enunciating what those principles are which seem to me to form the starting-point from which all architects should proceed.

Improved Hospital Construction in England may be said to date from the Report of the Royal Commission[1] on the Sanitary State of the Army, of 1857,

[1] This Commission consisted of the Right Hon. Sidney Herbert, Mr. Augustus Stafford, Sir Henry Storks, K.C.B., Dr. Andrew Smith and Mr. Alexander (late Directors-General of the Army Medical Department), Sir Thomas Phillips, Sir James Clark, Bart. M.D., Sir J. Ranald Martin, M.D., and John Sutherland, Esq., M.D.

presided over by the late Lord Herbert of Lea, which, for the first time, laid down those principles, without the observance of which no hospital can be kept thoroughly clean and healthy.

Amongst the first hospitals in which the principles so enunciated were practically embodied were those constructed according to the plans of the Commission[2] for improving Barracks and Hospitals of 1858, and illustrated in their report.

At a subsequent period similar principles, adapted more especially for India and other warm climates, were laid down by the Army Sanitary Commission in their suggestions for improving the sanitary condition of Indian stations, and are now being carried out in India. Since these reports[3] have been laid before Parliament similar principles of Hospital construction have been generally adopted in recent hospitals in this country and abroad.

[2] This Commission consisted of the late Lord Herbert of Lea (then the Right Hon. Sidney Herbert), J. Sutherland, Esq., M.D., Deputy Inspector-General of Hospitals Burrell, M.D., and the author of this address.

[3] Amongst the publications on this subject, Miss Florence Nightingale's works, and especially her "Notes on Hospitals," must be mentioned as having contributed largely to the spread of sound principles of Hospital construction in this and other countries.

ADDRESS.

A HOSPITAL or infirmary may be defined as a building intended for the reception and treatment of sick and injured persons, under conditions more favourable for recovery than such persons could otherwise command.

It follows as a necessary feature of hospital construction that the building should be so arranged as to enable a small staff of medical men, nurses, and assistants to minister to the necessities of a large number of sick. Now this can only be done by bringing many sick together in one establishment, and placing several sick in one room.

The first object of a hospital is that it should enable the sick to recover in the shortest possible time. It is now recognised by all that, in addition to skilled attendance, medicine, and food, the following are essential requirements for ensuring speedy recovery.

1. Pure air; that is to say, that there should be no appreciable difference in purity between the air inside the ward and that outside the building.

2. That the air supplied to the ward should be capable of being warmed to any required extent.

3. Pure water, and that it should be so supplied as to ensure the removal of all impurities to a distance from the hospital.

4. The most perfect cleanliness within and around the building.

In respect of this latter requirement, I may quote from the Report of Mr. Simon, the Medical Officer of the Privy Council, of 1864:—

"That which makes the healthiest house makes likewise the healthiest hospital : the same fastidious and universal cleanliness, the same never-ceasing vigilance against the thousand forms in which dirt may disguise itself in air and soil and water, in walls and floors and ceilings, in dress and bedding and furniture, in pots and pans and pails, in sinks and drains and dust-bins. It is but the same principle of management, but with immeasurably greater vigilance and skill; for the establishment which has to be kept in such exquisite perfection of cleanliness is an establishment which never rests from fouling itself ; nor are there any products of its foulness— not even the least odorous of such products—which ought not to be regarded as poisonous."

In order to give effect to these principles, it is necessary to consider:

1. The site of the proposed hospital.

2. The form of the rooms in which the sick are to be placed and nursed, so as to ensure purity of air and convenience of nursing; these rooms form the principal units of hospital construction.

3. The distribution of these units, and of the other necessary accessories, which when combined constitute the hospital.

1. Sites of Hospitals.

The local climate should be healthy; there should be nothing to prevent a perfectly free circulation of air over the district. There should be no nuisances, damp ravines, muddy creeks or ditches, undrained or marshy ground, close to the site, or in such a position that the prevailing winds would blow the effluvia arising from them over the hospital. The natural drainage outlets should be sufficient and available.

To test the healthiness of a site an inquiry into the rate of sickness and mortality in the district will afford valuable information as to its suitableness for sick. But care should be taken not to be guided by the mortality alone; for it by no means follows that a district with a low rate of mortality is suitable for sick. The nature of the diseases, and the facility, or otherwise, with which convalescences and recoveries take place, must also be taken into account.

The qualities of a site most favourable to a hospital in this country may be described to be a situation in the open country, upon porous and dry soil, with free circulation of air round it, but sheltered from the north and east; raised above the plain, with the ground falling from the hospital in all directions, so as to facilitate drainage.

No doubt it is impossible to secure a perfect site for every hospital, but in the construction of a hospital it will be necessary to discount any departure from these qualifications by increased floor space and cubic space for the patients, or by engineering arrangements outside the building,—that is to say, by increased expenditure.

But in any case the site selected for a hospital should not receive the drainage of any higher ground.

Clay soils and retentive soils generally should be as far as practicable avoided. It is an error to build a hospital on a steep slope. No doubt, by forming a plateau for the structure, and adopting a system of catch-water drainage, the water from the higher ground may be more or less cut off from the building; but the higher ground, especially if it be near to the building, and steep, and if it rise to a considerable height above the hospital, will stagnate the air just as a wall stagnates it. Shelter from cold, or from unhealthy winds, be it by means of a range of hills, or walls, or houses, or trees, should always be at a sufficient distance to prevent stagnation of air and damp, otherwise the shelter from an evil recurring only at intervals may be purchased by loss of healthiness at all other times.

Clear area upon which a Hospital should stand.

There should be no buildings near a hospital except those immediately connected with its object. As regards the minimum area upon which to erect a hospital, the Chirurgical Society of Paris in 1864 laid down as an axiom that the clear space in which a hospital should stand should not afford a less area than nearly 540 square feet to each patient,—that is to say, that a hospital for 80 patients should stand in the centre of an acre of ground; and they further said that the proportional area should be greater as the number of patients increases. In this country it has been held sufficient to allot an acre to 100 patients. There is, however, a limit to the number of sick which can be aggregated together on one site, and in one hospital, to which a further reference will be made.

2. Form and Distribution of the Parts of a Hospital.

After the selection of the site, the most important question is the structural arrangement of the building, which must be such as to secure free circulation of air.

Basis of Hospital construction is the Ward.

The basis upon which the structural arrangements rest is the ward. The first thing is to obtain good healthy wards; everything else, such as administration, means of access, and discipline, must be made subsidiary to the question as to how the sick are to get well in the shortest possible time, and at the least expense, and this, so far as the structure is concerned, is mainly determined by the form of the wards.

Conditions which regulate the size of Wards.

The size of a ward depends upon the number of patients which it should contain, and upon the cubic space and floor space which should be allotted to each patient.

Whilst the medical man prescribes for the sick, he depends for the execution of his orders upon the nurse. The nurse applies the remedies, gives food, and regulates the atmosphere, as an hourly continuous duty.

The disciplinary and economical dispositions in a hospital require that each nurse should have the patients allotted to her placed in one ward, under her immediate eye; and the head-nurse should be supreme in the ward which she nurses. Moreover, as economy of labour in administering the hospital is a main object to be sought in hospital construction, the hospital should be so laid out as to enable the largest number of patients to be nursed by a given number of nurses.

The number to be placed in a ward will therefore depend upon the number which can be efficiently nursed, and the form of the ward must be as much calculated to facilitate nursing as to ensure free circulation and change of air.

Miss Nightingale says that "a head-nurse can "efficiently supervise, a night-nurse can carefully "watch, 32 beds in one ward; whereas with 32 beds "in four wards, this is impossible." (Appendix to Report of Committee on Cubic Space in Metropolitan Workhouses; Paper on Nursing, by Florence Nightingale.)

Miss Nightingale further shows (in her "Notes on Hospitals," 1863) that if the annual cost of nursing be capitalized, and if a hospital for a given number of sick be divided into wards of nine patients each, the cost of nursing in perpetuity would be 428*l.* per bed : whereas if the hospital were divided into wards of 25 beds each, the cost would be 231*l.* per bed, and with wards of 32 beds, the cost would be 220*l.* per bed.

It has followed, from these considerations, that from 20 to 32 beds have been taken as the unit for ward construction. In hospitals where cases of more than ordinary severity are likely to be received, it would be necessary to diminish the size of the wards on grounds of health, and thus to make some sacrifice of economy of nursing for the sake of the patients.

Hence the actual ward-figure for each hospital depends on the nature, and to some extent on the size, of the hospital. Small wards are also required for occasionally isolating bad cases.

Conditions which regulate the form of Wards.

The general form of ward construction is the next consideration, and this is mainly governed by the question of the renewal of air.

Maintenance of Purity in the Air.

The purity of the air within an inhabited space, enclosed on all sides, is necessarily vitiated by the emanations proceeding from the bodies of those who inhabit it, and especially by the effect on it of their respirations. With persons suffering from disease, especially infectious fevers, or from wounds, or sores, these emanations are greater in quantity, and more poisonous in quality, than from persons in health. Stagnation in the movement of the air leads to rapid putrefaction of these emanations. If they diffused themselves uniformly throughout the space, as is the case with the carbonic acid which is thrown off from the body, ventilation would be comparatively simple, and, whatever the cubic space, the air would attain a permanent degree of purity, or rather impurity, theoretically dependent upon the rate at which emanations are produced, and the rate at which fresh air is admitted: hence the same supply of air will equally well ventilate any space, but the larger the cubic space, the longer it will be before the air in it attains its permanent condition of impurity, and the more easily will the supply of fresh air be brought in without altering the temperature, and without causing injurious draughts.

Upon the assumption that the impurities in a ward diffuse themselves equally throughout the atmosphere of the ward, the amount of air which should be removed, and its place supplied with fresh air, is at least 3,000 cubic feet per patient per hour; but this must depend to some extent upon the emanations of the patients, which vary with the diseases or injuries they are suffering from.

The number of patients in a ward varies from day to day, and the character of their diseases varies: hence the amount of impure emanations in a ward is variable.

On these considerations, it is advantageous to keep the ventilation of each ward independent of other wards or rooms; and, whilst ample means of renewing the air of the wards should be provided, yet these means should be under the supervision of some one in a position to be constantly aware of the ward requirements, and responsible for their being always efficiently maintained in action.

The change of air may be effected in various ways: for instance, the air may be drawn out by a fan; or it may be removed by a shaft whose action depends on the difference of the temperature of the air in the shaft and that in the outer atmosphere: of this the ordinary fireplace is one example; a sun-light is another example; a heated shaft connected with flues led from holes in the wall near the patients' beds, through each of which air is drawn into the shaft, is another example. The place of the air which is thus withdrawn is then taken by fresh air, which in cold weather must be warmed before it is passed into the ward if an equable temperature is to be maintained in the ward. Instead of withdrawing the air from the ward, fans or pumps, or (as Dr. Arnott proposed) a machine on the principle of a gas-holder, may be used to force fresh air into the ward, and thus to drive out the air previously in the ward.

It is thus quite possible so to arrange the ventilation mechanically that a specified quantity of air at a fixed temperature shall be forced into the ward by day and by night. Theoretically it would seem absolutely certain that, if a flue-opening were provided close to the bed of each hospital patient, and if the fixed proportion of air were drawn away by this flue, the whole of the emanations from the patients should go with it. But this is not so in practice. Unless the patient were enclosed in a case, part of the emanations would pass into the other parts of the ward. Moreover, mechanical ventilating arrangements are always to some extent more or less affected by variations in the temperature of the outer air and by the direction of the wind, and consequently require careful and constant supervision. Practically, hospitals dependent upon such means alone for ventilation have not been healthy. It may be that the process is not in accordance with Nature's mode of providing fresh air. To explain my meaning I cannot do better than quote from the remarks on the subject by Miss Nightingale. In her " Notes on Hospitals " she says :—

"Nature affords air both to sick and healthy of varying temperature at different hours of the day, night, and season ; always apportioning the quantity of moisture to the temperature, and providing continuous free movement everywhere. We all know how necessary the variations of weather, temperature, season are for maintaining health in healthy people. Have we any right to assume that the natural law is different in sickness ? In looking solely at combined warming and ventilation to ensure to the sick a certain amount of air at 60°, paid for by contract, are we acting in accordance with physiological law? Is it a likely way to enable the constitution to rally under serious disease or injury, to undercook all the patients, day and night, during all the time they are in hospital, at one fixed temperature? I believe not; on the contrary, I am strongly of opinion—I would go further and say, I am certain—that the atmospheric hygiene of the sick-room ought not to be very different from the atmospheric hygiene of a healthy house. Continuous change of the atmosphere of a sick ward to a far greater extent than would pay a contractor to maintain, together with the usual variations of temperature and moisture given by nature in the external atmosphere, are elements as essential as any other elements to the rapid recovery of the sick in most cases."

But there is also this consideration. The emanations from the body do not uniformly diffuse themselves ; they hang about as the smoke of tobacco may be said to do. In wards in which a fixed quantity of air is forced, there is not even a uniform degree of impurity; at times the air may be tolerably pure in one place, but very impure in another; consequently it seems to be necessary, in order to ensure the purity of the air of a ward, that means should exist for absolutely sweeping out all the impure air from the ward occasionally, and starting afresh with pure air. This is best effected by the direct action of currents of fresh air brought in by open windows placed on opposite sides of the wards. The distance between windows for this purpose must not be too great to prevent their efficient action in moving the air. Experience shows that a width of twenty-four feet affords very satisfactory results, but that opposite windows for such an object should in no case be more than from thirty to thirty-five feet apart. The space between the windows should not be obstructed by walls or partitions.

The same object renders it necessary to limit the number of patients—that is to say, the sources of impure emanations—placed between opposite windows to two.

In the Herbert Hospital the width of the wards is twenty-six feet: in the new St. Thomas's Hospital it is twenty-eight feet; and in the new Hôtel Dieu in Paris, twenty-nine feet; but these two hospitals are important medical schools. In the new Leeds Hospital, also a medical school, it is twenty-seven feet six inches.

In the day-time, and when the weather admits of

open windows, a ward with windows opening on both sides can easily be kept fresh; but for other seasons it is necessary to provide openings for the escape of impure air and for the admission of fresh air which shall not cause draughts.

The use of open windows is incompatible with the economical application of mechanical arrangements for renewing the air in wards; moreover, the ventilating requirements of each ward should be kept independent of those of other wards. This will be best effected by keeping a separate fire for each ward. If one fire is provided for each ward, it is best on other considerations to place it in an open fireplace in the ward.

The most powerful engine of ventilation for drawing out the air is an open fireplace. The way in which an ordinary open fireplace acts to create circulation of air in a room with closed doors and windows, is as follows.

The air is drawn along the floor towards the grate, it is then warmed by the radiating heat of the fire, and part is carried up the chimney with the smoke, whilst the remainder flows upwards near the chimney-breast, to the ceiling. It passes along the ceiling, and, as it cools in its progress towards the opposite wall, descends to the floor, to be again drawn towards the fireplace. It follows from this, that with an open fireplace in a room, the best position in which to deliver the fresh air required to take the place of that which has passed up the chimney, is at some convenient point in the chimney-breast, between the chimney-piece and the top of the room, for the air thus falls into the upward current, and mixes with the air of the room without perceptible disturbance.

In order to prevent the temperature of the ward from being lowered by the extraction of air, to maintain an equable temperature, and to prevent draughts, it is absolutely necessary to supply warmed air to replace that removed by the fireplace or by other openings. This may be done by placing coils of pipe, or flanged pipes, heated by steam or hot water, in convenient places, so as to allow the air drawn into the ward by the fireplace, or otherwise, to be warmed. But this plan is rendered unnecessary by the use of ventilating fireplaces,[1] constructed on the principle of those used in military hospitals and barracks: these fireplaces are constructed in such a manner as to utilize a portion of the heat generated by the fire, and which would otherwise pass away by the chimney, in warming fresh air which is admitted into the ward; and they are, besides aiding the ventilation in a remarkable degree, very economical of fuel.

In hospitals, arrangements should be made, either by providing gas jets in the chimney, or by warming the chimney-flue by means of an adjacent spare flue, to keep up a current in the chimney when the fire

[1] See Appendix.

is out; but it may almost be accepted as an axiom that, in this climate, when it is necessary to keep the windows closed, it is desirable to have a fire lighted.

It is not however sufficient, in this method of airing wards, to trust only to the fireplace and windows. In addition to the ventilation by means of the fireplaces, outlets for heated and impure air should be provided by means of shafts carried up from the ceiling to above the roof, which will act when the fire is out, and will prevent at such times stagnation in the upper part of the wards. The degree of action in these shafts depends upon the height of the shaft and upon the difference between the temperature in the ward and the temperature out of doors. I have found that an adequate change of air will not be satisfactorily obtained in all cases without a sectional area of at least one inch to every fifty cubic feet of space in the room for the upper floors, that is, immediately under the roof; of one inch to every fifty-five cubic feet in rooms on the floors below; and of one inch to every sixty cubic feet for rooms on the lower floors: but this to some extent depends on the heights of the rooms. It is preferable to allot these areas according to the cubic space in the rooms than according to the number of beds, because the number of beds may be varied according to the nature of disease; and the larger the cubic space necessary for a patient, the larger also should be the means of changing the air, because the permanent contamination of the air varies, not with the cubic space, but with the amount of fresh air admitted.

These shafts should, where the fireplaces are in the side walls, be placed if possible on the same side as the fireplaces; but if the fireplaces are in the centre of the wards, the shafts should be placed in the corners of the room furthest removed from the grates, as in that position they will be least liable to down draughts.

Each gas jet burning in the wards at night should be covered with a bottomless lantern connected with an extraction shaft or tube, so as to carry off the products of combustion; in wards which have the roof only above them, a gas sun-light, with direct communication with the outer air, is a convenient and powerful engine of ventilation.

Means for the admission of air of the ordinary temperature should be provided direct from the open air, independent of the windows and doors; for this purpose, Sherringham's ventilators should be placed between the windows near the ceiling, which should afford a combined area of at least one square inch for every hundred cubic feet of space in the room: eminent surgeons are of opinion that for bad surgical cases openings of equal size should be placed close to the floor under the beds, so as to allow the impure air to be swept out from under the beds, but these latter should be capable of being easily and securely closed, otherwise they create unpleasant draughts near the floor. The Sherringham ventilator placed near the ceiling admits the air without perceptible draught; but these ventilators will also be found frequently to act as outlets when they are open on the leeward side of a ward.

The simple methods of admitting air into, and removing air from, wards which I have here described, are those which after much consideration I have preferred to more mechanical and complicated methods, which might possibly be shown to be theoretically more perfect. But the theoretically perfect method of supplying a known quantity of air hourly into the ward, and neither more nor less, requires, if its action is not to be disturbed, that the windows shall not be opened, and that an open fireplace shall not be used. I believe, however, that health will be best secured by using open fireplaces, and by keeping the windows open when it is possible to do so, so as to sweep out the foul air, and introduce occasionally far more pure air than the quantity pronounced to be theoretically necessary. The inlets and outlets I propose are supplementary to the windows when these cannot be opened, and are not intended to supplant them.

All openings for the admission of fresh air should be capable of being easily examined and cleaned throughout their whole length, and should be thoroughly cleaned at least once a year.

Superficial Area per bed.

The next most important element in the question of ward construction is the superficial area to be allotted to the patients, for on this depend the distance of the sick from each other, the facility of moving about the sick, shifting beds, cleanliness, and other points of nursing. If there be a medical school attached to the hospital, the question of area has to be considered with reference to affording the largest amount of accommodation practicable for the teacher and his pupils.

A ward with windows improperly placed, so as not to give sufficient light, or where the beds are so placed that the nurse must necessarily obstruct the light in attending to her patients, will require a large floor-space, because the bed-space must be so arranged, and of such dimensions, as to allow of sufficient light falling on the beds. In well-constructed wards with opposite windows, the greatest economy of surface area can be effected, because the area can be best allotted with reference both to light and to room for work. Miss Nightingale, in her paper on the "Training of Nurses," in the Appendix to the Report of the Committee on Cubic Space in Metropolitan Workhouses, says that in an infirmary ward, 24 feet in width, with a window for every two beds, a 7 feet 6 inch bed-space along the walls would probably be sufficient for nursing purposes. This would give 90 square feet per bed, and there should be as little reduction as possible below this amount for average cases of sickness, but this space is much too small for fever or lying-in wards.

The practice in regard to area differs considerably in different hospitals. In the naval hospitals it is about 78 square feet per bed. In the Herbert Hospital, where there is no medical school, it is 99 square feet per bed. In the Royal Victoria Hospital at Netley, where there is a medical school, it is 103 square feet. In St. George's Hospital it is 69 square feet, a very small area for so important a school. From this minimum it varies to 138 square feet in Guy's Hospital. In the new Hôtel Dieu, at Paris, the space per bed will be from 104 to 110 square feet, and in the new St. Thomas's Hospital it will be 112 square feet. This latter area is considered sufficient both for nursing and teaching purposes. It will thus be seen that the question of area must be settled with reference to the existence or non-existence of a clinical school in the building and the number of pupils likely to follow the medical officer.

As the present paper refers exclusively to new hospitals, which we must suppose will not be constructed in unhealthy localities, we may fix the area at about 90 square feet per bed in this climate, with the understanding that the area shall be increased if the building is designed for a medical school, or where from unavoidable circumstances an unfavourable site must be selected.

Way in which the Space in a Ward should be laid out.

The next consideration is the allotment of the superficial area. The width between the opposite windows affords the limit in one direction, and convenience for nursing requires that there shall be a window near each bed: hence the superficial area must be so allotted as to afford convenient space for nursing purposes between the sides of adjacent beds, and between the feet of opposite beds.

If there is a window for each bed, the wall-space between every two windows should be six or eight inches wider than the bed, and in this case the width of the window, whatever that may be, would practically represent the distance between the beds. If there are two beds between every two windows, the distance between the adjacent beds of each pair of beds along the wall-space should not be less than three feet for facility of nursing.

If 7 feet 6 inches be set apart as the total linear space to be allowed for each bed along the side wall, this, with a superficial area per bed of 90 square feet, would give a ward 24 feet wide, which is a favourable width for ventilation; and, allowing a few inches between the bed-head and the wall, this width would give about 10 feet between the projecting ends of opposite beds.

Cubic Space resulting from these Conditions.

Assuming that these areas and distances are sufficient, then a ward height of 12 feet, which is scarcely sufficient except for small wards, would afford 1,080 cubic feet per bed. A height of 13 feet would allow 1,170 cubic feet, and a height of 14 feet, which is the height of the Herbert Hospital wards, would give 1,260 cubic feet.

Long wards require more height for efficient ventilation than short wards.

In a good situation, and for ordinary cases of disease and operations, those spaces which are enough for nursing and ward administration would, with good ventilation, be sufficient for all sanitary purposes; but for cases of severe fevers, such as typhus and other epidemic diseases, a much larger space and area would be required. In ordinary hospitals, when severe cases of this class come into the hospital, the simplest plan is to leave the bed adjacent to that occupied by the patient vacant.

It is, however, very much the practice to build special hospitals for these classes of cases. The aggregation of a mass of virulent emanations in one hospital, and in one ward, renders it necessary to provide a very large extent of floor-space and cubic space. This means very much increased expense for construction and nursing.

I am afraid that statistics go to show that special hospitals, where a number of fever cases are brought together, afford a higher death-rate than is due to the disease. These expensive structures cannot therefore be said to have secured the rapid recovery of the sick. Yet this class of cases is eminently that which should be treated in hospitals. Is it, however, desirable to aggregate all such virulent sources of emanations together in one ward in one hospital? Would it not be better to separate them amongst other patients in an ordinary hospital?

Whilst the mortality from this class of diseases is high in special hospitals, it is low in shed buildings, and even in no buildings at all. If, therefore, it be necessary to make special provision for epidemic disease cases, would it not be better to make such special provision in small hut wards, attached to ordinary hospitals, but separate from each other, and from the hospital proper? A simple, inexpensive hut for a few beds, capable of perfect ventilation, and admitting of being occasionally pulled down and rebuilt with fresh materials at no great expense, would in all probability afford more recoveries from fever and wounds than the most costly special hospital wards.

Materials for, and other details of, Ward Construction.

Having considered the principles which govern the size and general form of wards, the next point is the description of materials to be used for the walls, ceilings, floors, and windows.

With a view to economise heat in winter, and to keep the rooms cool in summer, the walls should be hollow, and all hospital wards should be ceiled, unless the roof is constructed of a good non-conducting material.

The best lining for a hospital ward would be an impervious polished surface, which, on being washed with soap and water, and dried, would be made quite clean. Plaster, wood, paint, and varnish all absorb the organic impurities given off by the body, and any plastered or papered room, after long occupation, acquires a peculiar smell. In a discussion in 1862, in the French Academy of Medicine, a case was mentioned in which an analysis had been made of the plaster of a hospital wall, and 46 per cent. of organic matter was found in the plaster. No doubt the expensive process which is sometimes termed enamelling the walls, which consists of painting and varnishing with repeated coats, somewhat in the manner adopted for painting the panels of carriages, would probably prove impervious for some time, but it would be expensive, and very liable to be scratched and damaged.

Parian cement polished appears to be the best material at present known for walls, but it is costly, and it can only be applied on brick or stone walls, and not on wood-work or partitions, because, being very inelastic, it is liable to crack. Cracks in a hospital ward are inadmissible, as they get filled with impurities, and harbour insects. The numerous joints required for glazed bricks, or tiles, render the use of these questionable as a lining for wards. The want of elasticity in Parian cement is unfavourable to its use in ceilings.

In default of Parian cement, which is costly, and which it is quite possible it may hereafter be found necessary to remove at distant intervals and replace with fresh materials, the safest arrangement is plaster lime-whited or painted, which should be periodically scraped so as to remove the tainted surface, and be then again lime-whited or painted. Of course these arrangements require the wards to be periodically vacated.

When plaster is used, it is essential, for the reasons before mentioned, that at the expiration of very few years the whole outer coat of plaster should be removed from the walls and ceilings, and new plaster substituted. The walls and ceilings should be quite plain, and free from all projections, angles, or ornaments which could catch or accumulate dust.

The floor should be as non-absorbent as possible, and for the sake of warmth to the feet it must in this country be of wood. Oak, or other close hard wood, with close joints, oiled and beeswaxed, and rubbed to a polish, makes a very good floor, and absorbs very little moisture. It is impossible to pay too much

CONSTRUCTION OF HOSPITALS. 25

attention to the joints: they should be like those of the best *parqueterie*, affording no inlet for the lodgement of dirt; for the impurities which become lodged in the cracks of a hospital floor are eminently objectionable. There should be no sawdust, or other organic matter subject to decay, under the floor. When one ward is placed over another, it is essential that the floor should be non-conducting of sound, and that it should be so formed as to prevent emanations from patients in the lower ward from passing into the upper wards.

The floors of the Herbert Hospital are formed of concrete, supported by iron joists, over which the oak boards are laid. An economical and non-absorbent surface for the floor can be obtained by first laying rough deal boards and covering them with thin, closely-laid oak boards. This floor should be cleaned like the French *parquet*, by *frottage*. A very good hospital floor is that used at Berlin, which is oiled, lacquered, and polished, so as to resemble French polish. It is damp-rubbed and dry-rubbed every morning, which removes the dust. Its only objection is want of durability. Both of the processes above mentioned render the floor non-absorbent, and both processes do away with the necessity of scouring, which is objectionable from the quantity of damp it introduces into the ward. The French floor stands the most wear and tear, but must be cleaned by a *frotteur*, which cleaning is more laborious than scrubbing, and does not remove the dust. The wet and dry rubbing process of cleaning above mentioned is far less laborious than either *frottage* or scrubbing, and completely removes the dust and freshens the ward in the morning. Practically, with care, a well-laid oak floor, with a good beeswaxed surface, can always be kept clean by rubbing.

All wood-work in a ward should be painted and varnished, so as to admit of easy washing and drying. The cleanest and most durable material is varnished light-coloured wainscot oak.

The form of the windows must be considered in their aspect of affording light as a necessary means of promoting health, of affording ventilation, of facilitating nursing, and of enabling the patients to read in bed. Light can always be modified for individual patients.

In order to give cheerfulness to the wards, and to renew the air easily, the windows should extend from within 2 feet or 2 feet 6 inches from the floor—so that the patients can see out—to within 1 foot from the ceiling. The windows should, as has been already explained, be placed on each side of the ward, with not more than two beds between each window, so that plenty of light may be thrown on each bed for facility of nursing. In wards affording about 1,200 cubic feet per bed, and with one window to two beds, the space between the end wall and the first window should be 4 feet 6 inches, and the space between the adjacent windows 9 feet, the windows themselves being 4 feet 6 inches wide, and the sides splayed about 6 inches on each side into the ward. An end window to a long ward is a great element of cheerfulness, and materially assists the renewal of the air at night.

It is essential to cleanliness that every part of the ward should be light. One superficial foot of window-space to from 50 to 55 cubic feet of space, will afford a light and cheerful room, but this depends much on situation and upon the walls being light-coloured.

As it is essential in this climate to economise heat in wards, with so much outer wall as the provision of windows on both sides requires, it is desirable to make the windows of plate-glass; double windows of ordinary glass would secure the same object and facilitate ventilation, but they are troublesome to clean, and almost always give a gloomy appearance to a room.

The best form of sash for ventilation in this climate is the ordinary sash, opening at top and bottom; but windows made in three or four sections, each of which falls inwards from an axis at the bottom of the section, have been extensively used in hospitals and possess many advantages; although I do not think that the air of the wards can be so thoroughly changed by means of these windows as by means of the ordinary sash.

Ward Offices.

The ward offices are of two kinds :—

1. Those which are necessary for facilitating the nursing and administration of the wards, as the nurse's room and ward scullery.

2. Those which are required for the direct use of the sick, so as to prevent any unnecessary processes of the patients taking place in the ward; as, for instance, the ablution-room, the bath-room, the water-closets, urinals, and sinks for emptying foul slops. There should, in addition to the bath-room here mentioned, be a general bathing-establishment attached to every hospital, with hot, cold, vapour, sulphur, medicated, shower, and douche baths.

Hot and cold water should be laid on to all ward offices in which the use of either is constantly required, because of the economy of labour in the current working of the hospital. For the same reason, when the wards are on two floors, lifts should be provided to carry up coals, trays, bedding, and even patients. Miss Nightingale (" Notes on Hospitals ") estimates that a convenient arrangement of lifts and laying on hot and cold water economises in attendance as much as one attendant to thirty sick.

Nurse's Room.

The nurse's room should be sufficiently large to contain a bed and to be the nurse's sitting-room. It

CONSTRUCTION OF HOSPITALS. 29

should be light, airy, and well ventilated, as a cheerful room is a material assistance to a nurse. It is necessary to discipline that it should be close to the ward door, and that it should have a window looking into the ward, so as to command it completely. If the nurse has two wards to supervise, her room should be placed between the two, with a window opening into each.

Ward Scullery.

There should be a ward scullery attached to each ward, and adjacent or opposite to the nurse's room, so as to be under her eye.

The scullery should be supplied with complete, efficient, simple apparatus for its various purposes; there should be a small range for ward cooking, so that the nurse can warm the drinks, prepare fomentations, &c. The best sink for washing up and cleaning the utensils is a white glazed fire-clay sink, with hot and cold water laid on. Care should be taken that the communication between the waste-pipe and the drain be made in the most careful manner, as hereafter described, otherwise foul air is certain to find its way into the hospital. Shelves or racks should be provided for ward cookery, but it is undesirable to have many cupboards or closed recesses for putting away things, as they become in time receptacles for dirt and rubbish. There should be no dark corners in the scullery, and it should have ample window-space. The scullery should be large enough for the assistant nurses to sit in, to have their meals comfortably.

There should be provided in, or adjacent to, the scullery or nurse's room, a hot closet for airing clean towels and sheets. For foul linen it is undesirable to have any receptacle near the wards, or indeed in the hospital building. It should all be placed in baskets, boxes, or trucks on wheels, and conveyed as soon as possible to the laundry. Ward sweepings and refuse should similarly be placed in moveable receptacles and taken out of the building with as little delay as possible; consequently I do not advocate any structural provision for the retention of these in or near the hospital.

Ablution Room, Water Closets, &c.

The ward offices of the second class ought to be as near as possible to the ward, but cut off from it by a lobby, with windows on each side, and with separate ventilation and warming, so as to prevent the possibility of foul air passing from the ward offices into the wards. They are therefore most conveniently placed at the end of the ward, furthest from the entrance and nurse's room; and distributed at each side, so as to enable the ward to have an end window.

The ablution-room should contain a small bathroom with one fixed bath of copper, supplied with hot and cold water. Terra-cotta when once warmed has the advantage of retaining the heat longer than almost any other material, and of being always cleanly, but it absorbs a great deal of heat at first. Hence when the bath is frequently used it is the best material; but if the bath is seldom used, then copper is better, or polished French metal.

A lavatory table of impervious material, such as slate or common white marble, with a row of sunk white porcelain basins with outlet tubes and plugs, each basin supplied with hot and cold water, should be placed in the same compartment as the bath, but separated from it by a partition and door. It is a common mistake to place these lavatory basins too near each other to be used conveniently by male patients standing abreast. It is undesirable to have closed receptacles under the basins, as they only accumulate dirt; nothing should be kept in these offices but what is required for constant use, and everything in use should be open to inspection. All fittings should be light-coloured, as they then show any want of cleanliness. There should also be room for a portable bath for each ward; this bath should be on noiseless wheels, and hot and cold water taps should be provided at a convenient height for filling, and there should be a sink on the floor level for running off the water out of the bottom of the bath after it has been used.

The water-closets should never be against the inner wall, but always against the outer wall of the compartment in which they are placed. A pan of a hemispherical shape, never of a conical shape, with a syphon, and abundantly supplied with water to flush it out with a large forcible stream, is by far the best contrivance for the water-closet of a hospital. The sink for slops, bed-pans, expectoration-cups, &c., which should have a compartment of its own adjoining the water-closets, should be a high, large, deep, round pierced basin of earthenware, with a cock extending far enough over the sink for the stream of water to fall directly into the vessel to be cleaned, and with an ample supply of water; this sink should be arranged to be flushed out like a water-closet pan. The space underneath should not be closed in; if it is, the enclosed part will be made a receptacle for rubbish. Walls of ablution-rooms and water-closets should be covered with white glazed tile, slate enamelled or plain, or Parian cement; plaster is not a good covering for them on account of their liability to be splashed, and of the necessity for the walls to be frequently washed down.

There should be private water-closets for the nurses, who should not use those of the patients; and also water-closets for the patients when not in their wards.

The ablution-room and water-closets should have plenty of windows opening to the outer air. They should have shafts carried up to above the roof, to carry off the foul air, and ventilating openings to admit fresh air independently of the windows, and warmed air should be supplied to them independently both of the wards and of the lobbies which cut them off from the wards, which latter should also be carefully ventilated and warmed separately. Care in these details is essential to prevent any of the air from these conveniences passing into the wards, especially in cold weather, and thus becoming a source of danger to the patients. All wood-work, such as seats to water-closets, should be of non-absorbent wood.

Drainage.

No drain should pass under any part of hospital buildings, because it is so difficult to ensure that brick or earthenware drains shall be kept permanently airtight in their whole length, and the smallest outlet may be a source of great evil; therefore all those appliances which are connected with drain-pipes, such as sinks, water-closet pans, &c., should be placed against the outside wall, so that the waste-pipes may be carried at once outside. They should also be placed under a window, so as to free them easily from smell should any arise, and to throw upon them abundance of light, and so avoid the accumulation of dirt. It is undesirable to build drain-pipes into walls.

Every precaution should be taken to prevent any drain smell from entering the building. The waste-pipes which convey away the refuse water should be all trapped just under the outlet from the basin, bath, urinal, or sink with which they are connected; they should pass into a waste soil-pipe, carried up to above the roof, and open at the top, so as to allow of an outlet for the gases displaced in the pipe when water is suddenly thrown into it from sinks or water-closets. This waste soil-pipe should be led into a trap at the bottom, to cut it off from the drain outside the building, and this outside drain should have a ventilation to allow of the escape of the gases generated in it, so as to prevent these gases from being able to force their way into the hospital. All such drain ventilation should be passed through charcoal filters.

Proportion of Ward Offices to Wards.

These ward offices will vary but little with the size of the ward; that is to say, a ward of twenty beds will require nearly as large ward offices as a ward of thirty-two beds. For instance, three water-closets per ward will suffice for a ward of thirty-two beds, but two at least will be required for even a twelve-bed ward. The superficial area to be added in the wards of thirty-two beds for these appliances would be about thirty square feet per bed, whereas in wards of twenty beds each it would come to nearly fifty square feet per bed. I point this out to show how much cheaper in first construction large wards are than smaller ones.

Unit of Hospital Construction.

The ward with its ward offices here described is the unit or basis of hospital construction. It is a

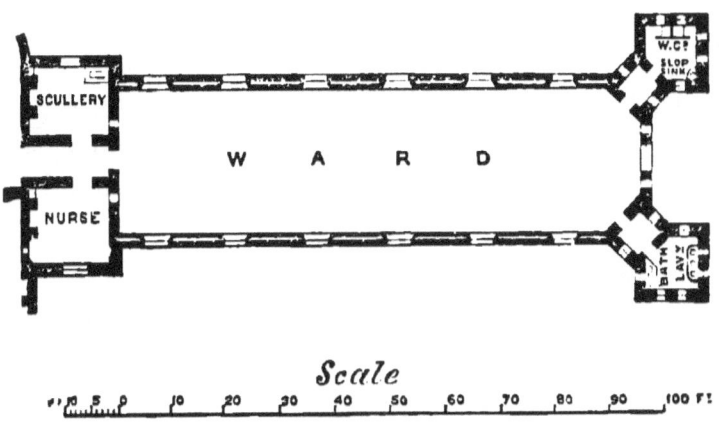

Fig. 1.—WARD AND WARD OFFICES.

small hospital, which may be increased to any required size by the addition of similar units.

3. Aggregation of Ward Units in the Construction of a Hospital.

The principles upon which these units of ward construction, or, as they are generally termed, pavilions, should be added, are as follow:—

1. There should be free circulation of air between the pavilions.

2. The space between the pavilions should be exposed to sunshine, and the sunshine should fall on

the windows, for which purpose it is desirable that the pavilions should be placed on a north and south line.

3. The distance between adjacent pavilions should not be less than twice the height of the pavilion reckoned from the floors of the ground-floor ward. This is the smallest width between pavilions which will prevent the lower wards from being gloomy in this climate; and where there is not a free movement of air round the buildings, this distance should be increased.

4. The arrangement of the pavilions should be such as to allow of convenient covered communication between the wards, without interfering with the light and ventilation, and therefore the top of the covered corridor uniting the ends of pavilions should not be carried above the ceiling of the ground-floor ward. Indeed, whilst it is necessary to make the ground-floor ward twelve to fourteen or fifteen feet high, it would be unnecessary for purposes of communication to give the corridor a greater height than from eight to nine feet, or possibly ten feet; there is however this consideration, that if the top of the corridor is made level with the ward-floors of upstairs wards, it affords a convenient terrace on to which the beds of patients can be wheeled, so as to allow them to lie in the open air. Each block of wards—that is, each pavilion—should have its own staircase.

5. No ward should be so placed as to form a passage-room to other wards.

6. As a general rule, there should not be more than two floors of wards in a pavilion. If there are three floors or more, the distances between the pavilions become very considerable, because of the rule, which ought to be absolutely observed, of placing the pavilions at a distance apart equal to at least twice the height of the pavilion, measured from the floor level of the ward nearest to the ground. Besides, when two wards open into a common staircase, there is, with every care, to some extent a community of ventilation. When there are as many as four wards one over the other, the staircase becomes a powerful shaft for drawing up to its upper part the impure air of the lower wards, which is then liable to penetrate into the upper wards. Similarly, heated impure air from the windows of the lower wards has occasionally a tendency to pass into the windows of the wards above. On these grounds, no hospital should have more than two floors of wards one over the other; and if there is a basement under sick wards, it should not be used for any purpose, such as cooking, from which smells could penetrate into the wards, and, when possible, it is best not to continue the staircase into the basement.

7. There is a limit to the numbers which should be congregated under one roof. This limit will depend very much on the nature of the cases. After considering well the experience of military hospitals, into

which many slight cases are received, it was decided that no more than 136 cases should be placed in one double pavilion, divided into two equal halves in such a way that the communication between the halves was cut off by through ventilation. In town hospitals, where the cases are of a more severe character, a similar double pavilion should probably not contain above 80 to 100 beds.

The size of any given hospital ought not to be determined by increasing the number of beds in any one building, but by increasing the number of units, each containing the numbers of beds I have mentioned; and the extent to which these units should be multiplied would, if the units have been properly constructed and arranged, be determined not so much by the number of patients as by considerations of economy in administering the hospital.

If economy in this matter were of no consequence, then any small number would answer, but in practice economy is best realized by increasing the number of beds up to the point at which a single administration can superintend them. This, Miss Nightingale says, might be done to the extent of 1,000 beds, but such an extensive hospital is not to be desired.[1]

Bearing in mind these principles, it may be accepted

[1] In the late American war some of the pavilion hut hospitals contained as many as from 2,000 to 3,000 beds. The statistics of recoveries in these hospitals, so far as I have been able to ascertain them, were not particularly favourable, but without an analysis of the cases it is impossible to say to what cause this was due.

as a rule that, so far as the sick are concerned, they would be better placed in wards all on one floor, opening out of a common corridor; and if land is cheap, and the site fairly level, it is probable that such an arrangement might be more economical than building two-storey buildings. The pavilions would be nearer together than in the case of wards on two floors, and consequently the distance to be traversed by the medical officers would be from twenty-eight to thirty feet horizontally between the pavilions in the case of the one-storey hospital, as compared with ascending from fourteen to sixteen feet by a staircase in the case of a two-storey building. On the other hand, the cost of drainage will be somewhat greater, and facilities for supplying hot and cold water to the ward offices will be less, in the one-storey hospital. On town sites it is absolutely essential to build hospitals as compactly as possible, and there is no doubt that economy in the current expenses will be best secured by a compact building with wards on two floors, provided with lifts and other labour-saving appliances.

In addition to the larger wards, it is necessary to have a few wards of one or two beds each for special cases; but these should be as few as possible, so as to economise labour in nursing, and their position must be adapted in each hospital to suit the arrangements of the principal wards, so as to afford easy supervision by the nurses.

It is moreover desirable that if convalescent patients remain in the hospital they should have rooms in which they can dine and spend the day apart from the other sick; the situation of these rooms should be such as not to interfere with the light and air of the wards. This class of patients also requires a chapel. It is, however, worthy of consideration whether, as a rule, patients who are able to move about in this way should be retained in hospitals; or, indeed, whether it would not be better to endeavour to establish convalescent institutions on the principle of the recently erected Atkinson-Morley Convalescent Hospital at Wimbledon, in direct and immediate connexion with a certain number of other hospitals. It is anticipated that this convalescent establishment will enable the authorities of St. George's Hospital to free their hospital beds in London much more rapidly, and thus receive many more patients in the course of the year; at the same time, it must be borne in mind that assemblies of mere convalescents present some disciplinary difficulties.

Arrangements for the several requirements above described must all be made subservient to the broad general principle of giving air and light to the wards.

All corridors connecting the wards should be kept as low as possible, so as not to impede the circulation of air between the pavilions; they should be lighted by windows on both sides, capable of opening wide, or of being removed altogether in warm weather, and they should be provided with ample means of ventilation, and supplied with fresh warmed air in cold weather.

The staircases should be treated similarly as to light and ventilation, and it is desirable to cut off the connecting corridors from adjacent staircases by swing-doors. These arrangements prevent draughts, and cause the passages and staircases effectually to cut off the ventilation of one pavilion from that of another.

The staircases for patients should be broad and easy; the rise of each step should not exceed four inches in height, and the tread should be at least one foot in width; there should be a handrail on each side, and a landing after every six or eight steps.

4. Administrative Buildings.

Having thus provided for the wards, the accommodation must be supplemented by the arrangements for what is called the administration.

The first point is to consider what is the smallest amount of this subsidiary accommodation which will suffice, and to provide that amount, and no more. Many rooms mean many servants, much cleaning, and consequent additional expense.

The necessary subsidiary accommodation may be briefly described as follows:—

1. Examining room, surgery and drug store, and

operating theatre; the latter should have roof-light from the north, and an airy operation ward should be placed near to it. A dead-house and post-mortem room should be provided, quite outside, and if possible detached from, the hospital. These rooms should be quite plain, and without projections or ornaments which would form a resting-place for dust.

2. Apartments for house-surgeon, matron, nurses, and servants.

The nurses should have airy bedrooms, with every accommodation for ablution, &c. attached, away from the wards, so that they may obtain pure air and complete rest while they sleep.

3. Stores for bedding and linen; kitchen; and provision stores.

The kitchen, and all those stores between which and the wards there is a constant movement, should be as central as possible, so as to save labour; but the kitchen should be carefully cut off from the corridor connecting the pavilions. The kitchen should be fitted up with adequate means of cooking rapidly and economically; the cooking apparatus should be adapted to cook a variety of food, and to secure the greatest digestibility and economy in the nutritive value of food: these are matters essential to recovery.

The hospital laundry should be detached from the hospital. Special care should be taken to make the buildings airy and very light, with ample means of ventilation for removing the steam, which is heavily charged with organic impurity, and with ample space for the washers. They should have separate drying and ironing rooms.

4. Those hospitals which afford outdoor relief require a dispensary for outdoor sick. This is in reality a separate establishment, and should always have an entrance separate from the hospital; indeed it might be detached except for the convenience of the medical men, and in order to have one drug store and one place for making up medicines. The extent of dispensary accommodation must depend entirely upon the local circumstances, and upon the extent and nature of the population to be accommodated.

The position and general construction of the administrative buildings should be made quite subservient to the accommodation for the sick, and to the broad general principle that they should not interfere with the circulation of the air round, or the light of the wards.

In order to ensure cleanliness and absence of smell, which are such material points in a hospital, it is essential that all these places, as well as all receptacles for brushes or pails, or for foul linen, should have ample windows opening direct to the open air, and be also ventilated by shafts carried up to above the roof of the building. I do not think that this point can be enforced too strongly upon the architect of a hospital. There should be no dark corners. Light means cleanliness.

5. Economical Considerations affecting Hospital Construction.

There remain to be said a few words on economy. I have shown how the size of wards may depend, to a great extent, upon economical considerations; that is to say, that if each ward is made to contain the largest number of patients which one head-nurse can effectually supervise, the number of nurses to be maintained will be reduced to a minimum, whilst if the patients be divided amongst several small wards, the number of nurses must be increased. The ward offices for a small ward of say twenty beds will nearly suffice for a much larger one. Therefore large wards are more economical than small ones, both in first construction and in current maintenance.

Again, if the ward walls are formed of an impervious polished material, which will allow of being cleaned by simple washing, and the floors are also impervious, the wards can be kept almost constantly full; whereas a ward with plastered walls must be periodically emptied to allow of their being scraped and cleaned; and hence a hospital with the cheaper form of wall-surface in the wards requires more wards to accommodate annually the same number of patients.

It is the same with the water supply, and the provision of other appliances for saving trouble to the attendants. The outlay for these things saves current expenditure by diminishing the number of attendants.

Again, the form of fireplaces or of cooking apparatus is very important, in order that economy of fuel, which also means saving of labour, may be obtained.

In deciding upon the first outlay these matters should be carefully weighed. Where a hospital is likely to be fully occupied at all times, it may be the truest economy to make it thoroughly complete with all labour-saving appliances, so that the current expenditure may be as small as possible.

The wards and ward offices form barely half the hospital. The administrative arrangements take up as much space again. Thus in a hospital for about 120 beds, I find that whilst there were allotted to the patients in the wards 1,200 cubic feet per bed, the cubic contents of the whole hospital amounted to nearly 2,800 cubic feet per bed.

Whilst it may be real economy to adopt somewhat expensive materials and other appliances in the wards, the same expense is quite unnecessary in the subsidiary accommodation, and thus saving may be effected.

6. Application of Principles to existing Hospitals.

Before considering how these principles have been applied in modern hospitals, I would point out one or two cases of hospitals where they have been eminently disregarded.

For instance, in King's College Hospital, situated in a very dense population, the wards are built round narrow courts, in a manner to preclude the free circulation of air; and instead of having windows to the open air on each side, the wards are placed back to

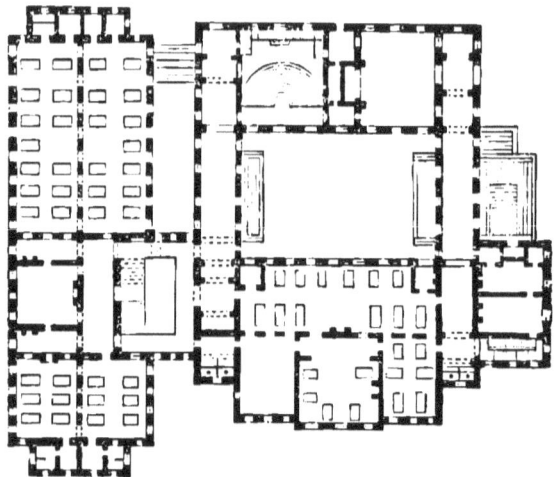

Fig. 2.—KING'S COLLEGE HOSPITAL, LONDON.

back, and the wards on one side have openings into each other, instead of into the open air.

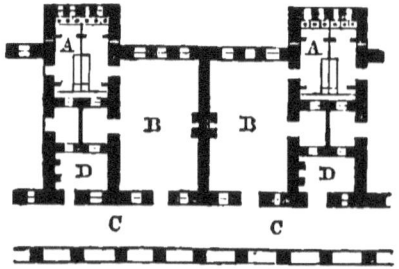

Fig 3.—WARDS AND WARD OFFICES AT THE ROYAL VICTORIA HOSPITAL, NETLEY. A. Water-Closets and Ablution Rooms; B. Wards; C. Corridor; D. Nurses.

In the Netley Hospital, the south side of the hospital is covered by a corridor which cuts off the fresh air from the wards on one side, and the circulation of air is impeded on the other side, where the ward windows open, by projections for the water-closets, &c. The nurses' rooms open only into the corridor, and the ward offices are not properly cut off from the wards.

Again, in Queen Charlotte's Lying-in Hospital, the building is an oblong, divided by a central passage, from which the wards open out on each side; the central wards have windows on one side only, and the impure air of the wards is liable to pass into the corridors and staircases, and permeate between the wards.

In the pavilion system this is an impossibility. The impurities of each ward are cut off from the other wards, and each pavilion becomes a separate hospital, in which the number of sick under one roof may be limited to any desired extent.

At the same time it must be borne in mind that the complement to the Pavilion system of the separation of the sick, is that the pavilions should be so arranged as to ensure circulation of air between the pavilions; if they are placed close together, and stagnant gloomy courts formed between them, they will not form proper hospitals for the recovery of the sick.

As an instance of defective pavilion construction I would adduce the Marine Hospital at Woolwich, in which the pavilions project from a central corridor, many of them on the north side. The wards are on three floors; the building containing the central corridor is carried up to the same height as the pavilions; the distance between the pavilions is not twice the height of the pavilions; consequently a gloomy hospital, without free circulation of air, and without the possibility of sunshine entering some of the wards, is the result.

A very important merit of the pavilion system is that it lends itself to almost any site. In its simplest form it would consist of one ward unit as above described, with a small ward and the necessary additions for administration. Such a hospital on one floor could accommodate from thirty to thirty-four patients. The ordinary regimental hospital for the army consists of two ward

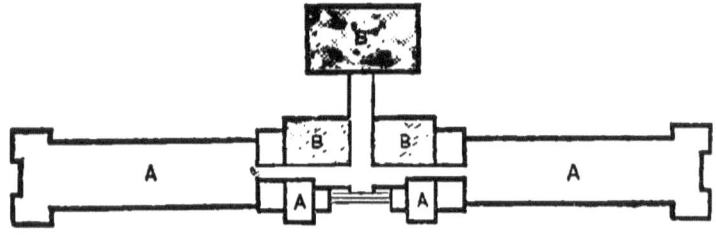

Fig. 4.—MILITARY REGIMENTAL HOSPITAL.
A A. Wards; B B. Administrative Department.

units or pavilions, united by the administrative offices, and with smaller wards carried out at right angles to the main line of building. The kitchen is placed behind and outside the building, separated by a covered corridor, with open sides. In order to ensure through light and ventilation to the centre of the building, the front of the administrative portion is retired behind the small wards, and there are three glazed arches in the centre, one of which is the door giving entrance to the hospital. In some cases these hospitals have wards on two floors, and contain 136 beds.

Very good examples of this comparatively simple form of pavilion hospital are also the Royal Hants County Hospital at Winchester, and the Buckinghamshire County Hospital at Aylesbury. A good illustration of the adaptability of the system to any site is

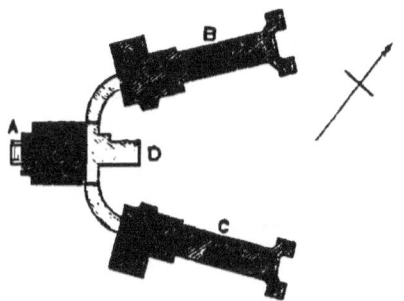

Fig. 5.—GENERAL PLAN OF SWANSEA NEW HOSPITAL.
A. Administration; B. Men's Wards; C. Women's Wards and Out-patients; D. Operating Room and Eye Ward.

afforded by the new hospital for 100 beds at Swansea, now in course of erection by Mr. Graham, architect. In this case the site is triangular, and the administrative block, operating theatre, &c., are placed at the apex of the triangle, which faces the prevailing wind, whilst the pavilions run down each side; and both sides of the wards receive sunlight and air.

I wish to call especial attention to this hospital, because it appears to me to embody most fully all the sanitary requirements I have enumerated, with great simplicity of form.

The hospital will accommodate 66 males, 32 females, and 2 eye-cases. The dispensary is designed to meet the requirements of a population of about 50,000, for the most part artisans and labourers. The provision for the nursing staff is ample: besides the three head nurses, accommodation is provided for nine day nurses and three night nurses. The floor space per bed is 100 feet; the cubic space 1,600 feet.

When larger hospitals are required, necessitating the adoption of several pavilions, they require in this climate to be united by a corridor. In hospitals of more than one storey high, this corridor should not extend above the ground-floor, consequently each pavilion must have its own staircase. In the Lari-

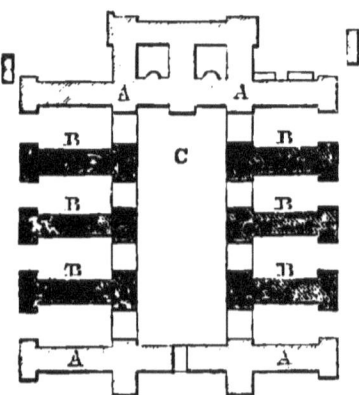

Fig. 6.—GENERAL PLAN OF THE LARIBOISIÈRE HOSPITAL, PARIS.
A A, Administration; B B, Wards for Patients; C, Courtyard.

boisière Hospital at Paris, the pavilions are parallel, and there are ten of them, of which five are on one side and five on the other side of a court, surrounded by an open arched corridor. The four outside pavilions are devoted to administrative purposes. The court is closed at the ends by buildings also connected with the administration, the chapel, and the baths.

There are three pavilions on each side for the sick; they have three floors of wards, to which access is given in each pavilion from the corridor by means of an easy staircase. The wards have no end windows, and the ward offices are not sufficiently cut off from the wards. The pavilions are only 64 feet apart, whilst the walls are 54 feet high.

The new hospital at Leeds is somewhat on the same plan, but the central court is narrower, and the pavilions, three in number, on one side of the central court, and two on the other, are solely occupied by the sick. They each contain two floors of wards. The hospital accommodates 350 patients. The administrative accommodation, including a dispensary for outdoor patients, is placed in the basement, above which the sick-wards rise. This is one of the newest of modern hospitals, and was built by Mr. Gilbert Scott. No expense has been spared in its construction. The corridors connecting the pavilions have a terrace roof raised above the level of the floor of the upper wards, and a glass roof which rises almost as high as the roofs of the upper wards has been placed over the central court. This tends to prevent the free circulation of air in the central court and adjacent corridor, and the height of this roof and of the terrace

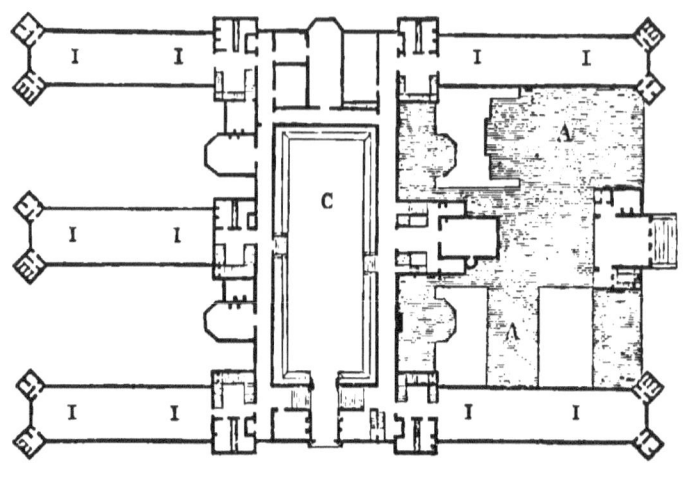

Fig. 7.—GENERAL PLAN OF NEW HOSPITAL AT LEEDS.
I I, Wards for Patients; A A, Administration; C, Courtyard.

above the corridor may somewhat stagnate the air in the courts between the northern pavilions.

In the Vincennes Hospital there are four pavilions joined by twos together to a central staircase. These pairs of pavilions so united are parallel to each other, and each pair forms one side of a square, the upper end of which is closed by a block of building for administrative purposes, including kitchen and other appurtenances. There are four floors of wards, which are certainly too many, and there are no lifts; consequently the administration of the hospital is laborious.

CONSTRUCTION OF HOSPITALS.   53

The Herbert Hospital affords another illustration of the method of uniting pavilions in twos, end to end; but in this case the staircases are, as it were, strung on to the corridor, which is purposely kept low between the double pavilions, so as to allow the sunshine to reach the space between the pavilions on the north of the corridor. In the centre the pavilions

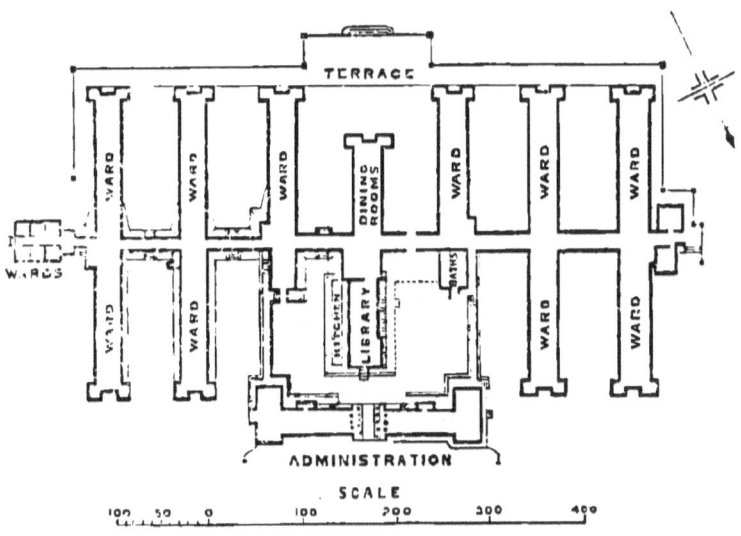

Fig. 8.—GENERAL PLAN OF HERBERT HOSPITAL, WOOLWICH.

are single, and placed on the south side of the corridor, and the central space on the north side is occupied by the administrative offices. The principal part of the service of the hospital is carried on in a basement passage, so as to avoid interference with the ward floors. This arrangement, whilst strictly adhering to sanitary principles, reduces to a minimum the distance to be traversed in proceeding from the central part to every other part of the hospital.

Fig. 9.—SKETCH OF THE ENDS OF THE SOUTHERN PAVILIONS OF THE HERBERT HOSPITAL, SHOWING THE ELEVATION OF THE CENTRAL CORRIDOR.

Cost of some existing Hospitals.

The Leeds Hospital accommodates 350 patients, and cost 197*l.* per bed. The Herbert Hospital accommodates 650 patients, and cost 320*l.* per bed; but of this expense at least 150*l.* per bed was due to the peculiar site, which necessitated at one end an extensive removal of earth to obtain a platform, and at the other the construction of an expensive basement, so as to place the wards on a level.

The Royal Hants County Hospital cost, exclusive of the chapel, land, and incidental expenses, 229*l.* per bed. This amount includes accommodation for out-patients, and provides 108 beds.

The actual cost of the Swansea Hospital, including the out-patients' department, was 142*l.* per bed, but the space occupied by the dispensary and out-patients' department is equivalent to thirty beds, so that if the hospital were for in-patients only, the cost would be 109*l.* 10*s.* per bed. It is quite certain that, with care and attention to economy in the design, there is no reason why a hospital for in-patients only on a favourable site should exceed from 90*l.* to 120*l.* per bed.

Conclusion.

I am unable, in an address limited for time as this one necessarily is, to do more than glance at the general principles of hospital construction, but I must point out that it is in their detailed application that so many errors are committed.

The architect should make his whole design subservient to these principles; he should be permeated by them; his watchwords should be—light, air, speedy removal of refuse, and great facility of cleansing.

The smallest number of parts compatible with the requirements of the hospital should be arranged in the simplest form, and solely with reference to the wants of the patients, and to the way in which the service can be carried on with the smallest number of attendants.

The architecture should be an expression of the need, and nothing more. Any sacrifice of sanitary requirements to architectural features is wrong; it adds uselessly to the cost. Ornament means too frequently the creation of corners and projections, which delay and stagnate the air, and form receptacles for dirt; it means present outlay and continual cost in repairs.

While so much suffering remains unprovided for in

the world, it is melancholy to see a large portion of the money which has been gathered with so much difficulty for the relief of that suffering diverted from its main object, in order to create a monument of the architect's taste.

I would add one more caution. Do not build for a long futurity. Buildings used for the reception of sick become permeated with organic impurities, and it is a real sanitary advantage that they should be pulled down and entirely rebuilt on a fresh site periodically.

I trust I have not trespassed too much on your time. The hospital is the handmaid of the physician. If he is to cure disease, he must place the patient in conditions to enable Nature to do her part, not in conditions which would thwart both nature and all the art which the physician can bring to bear.

These conditions it is the part of the medical man to lay down. My part has been to endeavour to show how the architect must shape his building so that it shall be in accordance with what the physician has declared to be necessary.

To the world in general the question I have discussed is technical and dry, but to you, whose daily life is spent in efforts to allay the sufferings of your fellow-creatures, it is fraught with deep interest ; and my only regret in coming before you to-day is that you have not had a more efficient exponent of this important subject.

DISCUSSION.

Dr. Evory Kennedy (of Dublin), in opening the discussion, said that he was extremely gratified with Captain Galton's most instructive and comprehensive paper, and that he could not conceive the question discussed in it put more fairly and practically. Ventilation had hitherto occupied our attention as the great question in connexion with our hospitals, and a great question it ought to be. The necessity that existed in hospitals for special arrangements and provisions to secure the exhaustion and re-supply of air throughout the wards and passages could not be overrated, and every improvement such as is so well insisted upon in Captain Galton's paper should be adopted to carry out these objects, and especially the primary one of exhausting the chambers and passages. When this was effectually accomplished, the re-supply of pure air followed as a matter of course. But even admitting that all the most approved appliances were rendered available; with this object he agreed fully with Captain Galton that they would be well supplemented by the presence of the ordinary chimneys, and that additional advantage would be derived from them, no matter what other plan for ventilating was adopted. Dr. Kennedy regretted, however, Captain Galton having sanctioned by his authority the construction of Pavilion Hospitals on the principle adopted at Leeds, St. Thomas's, and elsewhere, provided an interspace of only double the height of the building was given. The proximity of the blocks, admitted to be a defect in the Lariboisière Hospital in Paris, was corrected to a certain extent in St. Thomas's, where Mr. Curry allowed an interspace of 125 feet between the blocks generally, and of 200 feet in the centre court; but in all these new structures Dr. Kennedy thought a' principle of extreme importance had been lost sight of as a means of securing the exhaustion and change in the stagnating air of the hospital wards, namely, the influence of the external atmospheric currents; parallel blocks necessarily holding a mass of stagnated air between them, and thus intercepting and precluding the operation of the currents. It was attention to this important matter that, in his mind, rendered the Swansea Hospital with its divaricating blocks of pavilions much preferable; and hospitals conducted on this plan, especially where the approximating ends of the blocks are, as far as practicable, detached from one another, so as to permit of a free transmission of currents throughout the whole line of each block, must necessarily prove more healthy. Although at the Leeds and St.

Thomas's Hospitals it is now too late to correct this grave defect, there are defects, particularly in the construction of the former, quite remediable, and which Dr. Kennedy did not doubt the managers would rectify on the first attack of erysipelas, pyæmia, or hospital gangrene with which they may be visited. He alluded to the closed corridors and the magnificent glass-covered court or winter garden in the centre of the building, and to which access existed from all the wards *under cover*. The simple removal of the windows in the corridors would do much for purifying the atmosphere of the hospital, and securing currents in the present stagnating mass of air that necessarily pervades the wards. But the massing all the wards of the hospital into a common atmospheric mass, having every part of it loaded with every miasm or poison that may originate in any part of the building, is so palpable a mistake, that when once zymotic disease shows itself, the glass roof must be removed, the corridors opened by the removal of the windows at least; and thus an approximation to that isolation that ought to have been kept in view in the original structure, and which has been thus marred, may be established. Dr. Kennedy thought, however, it would be a great pity that the winter garden should be lost to the patients; its advantages might be continued to them by removing it to a vacant piece of ground which, he understood, belonged to the managers, close to the hospital, and connecting the two by a covered way. He remarked that another and not less important subject to which Captain Galton had called attention, and with his observations on which he (Dr. Kennedy) had been much struck, was that conveyed in the latter part of Captain Galton's paper, upon the existence in hospitals of organic impurities, and the necessity of their removal and future prevention. His observations upon the use of Parian cement upon the walls and ceilings, as well as the objections urged to angles and corners, were valuable. None of these hints should be lost sight of in our new structures, and even ought to be applied, when practicable, in correcting the defects of our old buildings. We were still in our infancy in our investigation of those laws which bear upon hospitalism, and yet the Jews were familiar with some of those practical influences that were only now opening upon us. He referred to what is said in Leviticus xiv. 39—45, upon the Jews cleansing the walls of their houses infected with leprosy by scraping and purification, and, if necessary, removing altogether out of their cities the materials of their stone houses. There existed, no doubt, a miasmatic atom or germ which, although so minute and impalpable as to escape our detection as yet, and which ventilation cannot reach, yet adheres to the walls, charges the atmosphere, and even permeates the solid structure of a hospital. This poison it is that constitutes hospitals, as is seen, the *habitat* or residence of certain zymotic diseases, some of which, as metria, pyæmia, and hospital gangrene, are rarely seen out of them. It works often for a considerable time latent, until the law of cumulation develops it into a more active or poisonous state; and eventually a state of complete saturation is arrived at. The poison or miasm is now so confirmed that the disease which was in the first instance perhaps due to self-poisoning or sporadic laws, or may have been contracted secondarily, becomes now a hospital disease or pure endemic. When this is the case, the disease spreads and actually destroys from a susceptible person being simply exposed to the atmospheric or endemic poison that pervades the hospital; and patients who resort to these institutions for the cure of minor and curable ailments are struck down with a disease very destructive, nay generally fatal, in its character. In conclusion, Dr. Kennedy added that great obscurity had hitherto enveloped the inquiry into these hospital diseases; however, public attention had now been called to them, and when it became generally known that the three principles he had insisted upon, and had elsewhere fully treated of under the terms *habitat*, *cumulation*, and *saturation*, were actually in daily operation in many of the great hospitals throughout Europe, and that a large proportion of our hospital mortality is due to the *defects in the construction of these buildings* into which we invite the sick to resort; when these facts became generally *known*, the first step, in his opinion, had really been taken towards the correction of a gigantic evil. In short, he had *no doubt* but that effectual means would be forthwith taken by all concerned to lessen an unavoidable mortality, now that the removal of its chief cause was shown to be within our own control.

MR. JONATHAN HUTCHINSON (London) had been connected with four hospitals, and for some years he had taken great interest in this question. The four hospitals with which he had been connected represented different management, and were built on different plans. One with which he had been connected for six years was badly managed as regarded accommodation, but the most successful as regarded treatment. He differed a little from some of the principles at present in vogue as to hospital construction and hospital dangers; but he would state his own great appreciation of the able and very excellent paper which Captain Galton had read, and he would also refer with admiration to the zeal and energy of Sir James Simpson in carrying on his work. But he could not help feeling exceeding doubt as to a movement which had taken so strong a hold upon the public mind. He felt that the notion was wrong that hospital efficiency was increased by increasing ventilation. In his opinion it was not the quantity of air, but the freedom from the germs of organic disease, which should be the chief desideratum. Just as the physician dealt with the germs of contagious disease, so the surgeon should be prepared to deal with septicæmia, erysipelas, and hospital gangrene. If he had time, he could give strong evidence that these diseases spread by contagion, and would spread in hospitals, but would stop if the cases were separated. Fresh air only diluted the germ—it did not get rid of it. This led to a very important question as to how hospitals might be built; and he thought he could rightly say that nine-tenths of the cases admitted might be taken into any kind of hospital and do equally well. Three-fourths of the surgery cases were simple fractures, and in cases in which there was no risk of contamination. Extra precautions had to be used in a small minority of the cases; and there need not be that large expenditure as to many of them which was entailed under ordinary circumstances; but when there were huts to resort to, he found there was no special risk of contagious disease. Then, as regarded ventilation, he really could not see, from experience, that increase of ventilation materially diminished the risk. He believed that in some ways it increased it. He did not believe that hospital gangrene was influenced by ventilation. If in hospitals there were one ward which had no communication with others, there would be no case of hospital gangrene. Such was the result of the evidence afforded in the London Hospital, with which he was connected. Their experience of epidemics was that, though they had none for six or seven years, at last there was a violent outbreak. He appealed to every hospital surgeon whether it was not the testimony of nurses and patients alike that too great ventilation acted injuriously, and was fraught with danger. Nurses said that, if they had the chance, patients would shut the windows. He (Mr. Hutchinson) coincided with that prejudice of the patients, and was not astonished that there were so many cases of bronchitis contracted by patients when lying in bed, because of the draughts from the open windows blowing right down upon them. Then there was an interesting suggestion which might modify their future belief as to the causes of mortality in hospitals. All the while that they were studying the ventilation of hospitals, they were using numerous specific agents for disinfection. Take the palatial institution built in Leeds—a finer institution as regarded comfort he never had the opportunity of seeing. But he should look with great interest at the statistics of the next ten years as compared with the statistics of the last ten years of the old and badly-ventilated building which had just been abandoned. It was possible that in the future there might be a great diminution in the number of cases of septicæmia and erysipelas; but he thought it could not be seen that any great improvement had been made in the isolation of contagious diseases. He had himself seen some small wards used for that purpose. The contrast between the next ten years and the past might be fallacious. Some might say it was due to ventilation, while all the while it might be owing to the employment of carbolic acid. Carbolic acid might possess a virtue which a circulation of air did not; and it was one of the most important points, whether the vapour given off from carbolic acid could or could not destroy the germs of specific disease. If it could, it would save a great deal of cost.

SIR JAMES SIMPSON was not opposed to hospitals, but he was against hospitals as at present constructed; and he thought they required very great reform. Most gentlemen in the room knew the test which had been applied by various writers latterly in reference to the mortality in the hospitals—viz. taking the results of the major amputations of the limbs, —that is, of the thigh, the leg, and arm and forearm— as a test of the healthiness of the different institutions. He had had now upwards of 6,000 cases of limb-amputation reported to him, the results of a portion of which were published, but others were not yet completed. Of these results he had only calculated some lately. Captain Galton had not alluded to the size of hospitals, but that seemed to be a matter of very great moment. In the large Parisian hospitals, one man out of every one and a half died when the limbs were amputated—three out of every five—a terrible mortality. When they came to

F

Britain, they found that in the hospitals that had more than 300 beds the ratio was not so great as one in one and a half, but still the mortality was frightful; it was one in two and a half. He had obtained the statistics of about 2,000 patients in provincial hospitals; and there he found that of hospitals that contained less than 300 beds and down to 150, the mortality was one in four, greatly less than in London. When they came down to hospitals with from 150 to 25 beds, the mortality was about one in five or five and a half; and when they came to cottage hospitals, the mortality was only one in seven. But further, in country practice, when the patients were isolated and each placed in a separate room, the mortality in the four limb-amputations was, amongst practitioners in general, only about one in nine; and where the country surgeon was in the habit of operating, it was found that the mortality diminished to one in twelve. Patients in the country were treated in their own dwellings or isolated rooms, and the question was, seeing that the patients recovered in a proportion so immensely greater in poor cottages than in rich hospitals, should not our great hospitals be changed from palaces into villages, from mansions into cottages? An architect could construct for the purpose a splendid village as well as a splendid palace. Or, for humanity's sake, shall we—if this reform is totally resisted—be driven to yet another alternative,

DISCUSSION.

viz. instead of having operative cases sent from the country into city hospitals, why should not the patients in our city hospitals requiring any serious operation be sent, for their own sakes, into the country village and cottage, to be submitted there to the surgeon's knife? The day before he left Edinburgh he had received a letter from a gentleman who was one of the grandest specimens he ever knew of an accomplished country doctor. He alluded to Dr. Dewar, sen., who formerly practised at Dunfermline, and was beloved and respected by all. This practitioner, though living within fifteen miles of Edinburgh, had never sent a case to any infirmary; and, although he could not state definitely the number that came under his care, he was certain they exceeded fifty; perhaps, in all, they amounted to fifty-three. Of these fifty all recovered except one, and that also would have recovered but for removal on the ninth day. Supposing these fifty cases had been sent to the nearest large hospital, instead of one death there would have been twenty, taking the usual average of deaths from limb-amputation in such institutions. He was inclined to think that a building of one storey was probably the best plan for hospitals; and that, in time, all would come to that opinion. He noticed the results of the Commission appointed to inquire into the health of barracks; and which held that all stables for Her Majesty's cavalry should henceforth be built of a single storey, with no sleeping-places and residences for men overhead. They unanimously came to this conclusion, after due examination, because they found such stables were the healthiest and safest for the horses, and horses cost some 30*l*. apiece. But what in this respect is healthiest and safest for the horse is no doubt the same for the sick man. Then, commenting on the construction of the Leeds Hospital, he stated that probably the roof in the central garden would yet require to be removed, and that the windows in the corridors should be taken out in order to effect proper ventilation. He also observed that if they would take the windows out of the enormous staircase in King's College, and let the air pass in freely, it would probably make it a far more healthy hospital. In a conversation with the matron at the Leeds Hospital, he found that she had been at St. Thomas's Hospital, London, and she told him that they only sent to the iron cottage hospital, which existed in the grounds there, "extreme cases" which were not likely to recover elsewhere. But if, he urged, "extreme cases" were sent for recovery to this cottage hospital, why should other cases be denied the same benefit, and the hospital be made entirely of cottages? Captain Galton had spoken of putting up barracks for treatment. In Germany, that was done at this hour; and the benefit of such hospitals had been felt during the late war between

Prussia and Austria. He did not say the palaces should be given up, but he thought they ultimately would, and, in the meantime, a great revolution should probably be made in them. For, modifying their present hospitals, it might be thought worthy of consideration that they should adopt Sir Sydney Waterlow's plan in regard to dwellings for the artisans of London; namely, that they should divide each flat so that it does not communicate with another flat except by a staircase perfectly open to the external air—and that each flat or landing has for itself a separate open balcony from which the tenements on that flat separately enter. Perhaps by building up all those doors in the wards of our present mansioned hospitals which open upon the staircases, and by using the staircases only as means of reaching external balconies to each flat or ward, much could be done to isolate entirely the individual wards, making each of them self-ventilated, and preventing the air from them all commixing in the common staircases and corridors, and re-entering wards in more or less of this foul state. We might thus perhaps change a large mansioned hospital into a series of cottage wards—perfectly separate in their ventilation from each other. The matters expired and exhaled, and the discharges from patients and their wounds, did not only affect more or less the patients in the same ward—and hence the great advantages of isolation—but even those in other wards which it could reach by common staircases and corridors. Dr. Rumsey had just informed him, for example, of the fœtid effluvia arising from a hepatic abscess being smelled, when the abscess was opened, by patients placed in wards at a very great distance along the corridor in the hospital at Netley. Other exhalations and effluvia —though not thus traceable by their fœtidity— passed doubtlessly from ward to ward, and affected more or less diseased human beings when they were aggregated together. The time, often minutes, properly allotted to each speaker, prevented him discussing what he had long ago written upon, viz. the probable diffusion by contagion, alluded to by Mr. Hutchinson, of some forms of surgical fever or pyæmia; just as some forms of puerperal fever spread by inoculation and contact; but in reference to Mr. Hutchinson's remark, that the use of carbolic acid might possibly prevent this mischance, and reduce the danger of operations, he would beg to state that in the great hospitals of Glasgow and Edinburgh the mortality from amputations, as shown by their statistics, had not decreased, but the reverse, since carbolic acid began to be used, and the number of deaths from compound fractures was increased, and not diminished.

DR. RUMSEY (Cheltenham) said he rose to state a little more in detail a fact to which Sir James Simpson had alluded. Two or three months ago he went over the magnificent hospital at Netley, and was at once struck with its grand defect—namely, that all the wards were erected parallel and in close juxtaposition, so that there was no possibility of thorough ventilation, except by means of the long corridor into which they all opened. As showing the defect of the corridor system, he was informed by one of the professors that, in a case of hepatic abscess, which contained highly fœtid pus, and had been opened in a ward at the extreme end of the corridor, the first announcement that the horrible smell was perceived in the hospital was made, loudly enough, from a ward at the other end of the corridor, a third of a mile distant, showing that the putrid air had been carried by the corridor to that distance. He thought a stronger condemnation of the corridor plan, and of the side-by-side construction of wards, to which the corridor gave access, could not be brought forward. It was a most important element in the construction of pavilion hospitals that the pavilions, instead of being parallel, should diverge, as was the case at Swansea. He wished that Dr. Oppert were here present, for that gentleman could have described to them the construction of the Alexandrow Hospital at St. Petersburg,—the pavilion wards of which spring from a polygonal corridor, and diverge very widely from alternate facets of the polygon, at a greater angle than those at Swansea, and therefore allow of a much freer circulation of air between the pavilions.

Dr. Stewart (London) said he had been at Netley, and found that, owing to the frequent prevalence of cold blustering weather, the windows for the most part were kept closed. Ventilation had been found almost impossible, owing to the high winds which frequently prevail. Having gone repeatedly over the wards, he had asked the attendants how they managed to keep them in a healthy state. They replied that they did the best they could, but it was a matter of difficulty. It had been pointed out to the Commission entrusted with the construction of Netley Hospital, that the corridor was utterly offensive, and that it would be impossible to keep any effluvia from permeating the whole of the wards. Some alterations in the plan were made, but the worst objection was carried through. A motion was brought forward by Mr. Sidney Herbert in reference to this hospital, recommending that it should be given up altogether. Unfortunately, the question of construction was mixed up with that of the site, which was a good one; and those in favour of the construction, by showing what an admirable site it was, managed to gain the attention of the House of Commons, and succeeded in turning the building into a hospital after all. They represented that it was not intended to be properly a hospital, but only a convalescent home; but, when the hospital came into use, so many large parties of soldiers constantly coming home were sent to it, that the hospital was generally very full. He might mention that the corridor was a close one.

Dr. HUGHES BENNETT (Edinburgh) said that he feared he belonged to that comparatively small section of the profession that desired to base its knowledge on the sure foundation of unquestionable truth, rather than upon vague opinion and fallacious assumption. We were constantly hearing all kinds of hypotheses advanced, unsupported by the slightest research or proof. Hence his anxiety for the appointment of committees, with grants of money, which would enable them to settle positively doubtful points in medicine. What they had just heard, and what they were constantly hearing, as to the construction of hospitals, was a good illustration of professional discussions. The cause of epidemics and endemics, it must be admitted, was as yet unknown, and constituted one of the most difficult investigations it was possible to enter upon; yet the most contradictory opinions regarding it were now brought forward, in order to influence the structure of hospitals. The medical department of the Royal Infirmary of Edinburgh, of which he was a physician, was one of the best ever planned; and, so far as he knew, no epidemic had ever originated in it. It was a model hospital; but it was now so old that its walls could no longer stand, and they were about to replace it by a new one. Those walls, however, were as capable of absorbing organic germs and miasmata as those of any similar institution; yet no harm had resulted. For a long time it was maintained that free ventilation was the best remedy for preventing the spread of disease in hospitals; but they had just heard a speaker maintain that ventilation was more injurious than beneficial, and that the constant open windows produced worse maladies than those which it was intended in this way to remove. While opposed, however, to the theory of free ventilation, he adopted the revived and fashionable hypothesis of "organic germs," and their destructibility by means of carbolic acid. But had any one seen these germs? or had they any existence except in the imagination? Our modern microscopes enabled us to examine particles much more minute than the smallest vegetable spores or animal ova. Surely, then, those who attributed to germs the origin of numerous diseases, and sought to modify the construction of hospitals because of their influence, should at least take some pains to find them and show them to others. No one, however, had done this. There was no proof whatever that such germs had any reality; and yet here was a large body of scientific and medical men considering how to build hospitals, and probably waste thousands of pounds in order to prevent the evils of such imaginary existences. Then statistics were had recourse to, on which to form conclusions; and these also were too frequently only assumptions. Sir J. Simpson had adopted deaths from amputations as a test of hospital mortality. Without impugning the facts brought forward, should we consider the test a good one? He (Dr. Bennett) thought not. Other causes influenced the results of amputations, besides the badness of hospitals. The inhabitants of large towns, for example, such as Manchester and Leeds, were more liable to sink under the shock of such operations, than the robust labourers in the country. As an example of the assertions so constantly advanced instead of proof, he might refer to the statement that a country practitioner had had fifty amputations with only one death. But they had also been told that that practitioner had lost his notes; and, if so, little confidence ought to be placed in such an assertion, when the point to be ascertained was the ratio of the dead to the survivors. Medical men were very apt, from memory, to exaggerate the number of their successful cases. What was required were carefully-taken records to determine with exactitude the nature of the case and the results of treatment. He therefore considered it advisable, in all medical investigations, to abolish such vague generalities, and in future seek to advance medical knowledge and practice on the indisputable grounds that scientific investigation alone could furnish.

Dr. George H. B. Macleod (Glasgow) said he would not have ventured to address the meeting but for the remark that had been made by Sir James Simpson regarding the high mortality attending operations in the hospital to which he was surgeon. The Infirmary of Glasgow was placed in the midst of a very dense population, in the oldest part of the town, and part of the house was old and not well constructed. The cases admitted into the wards were often very severe—in fact, as severe as it was possible to conceive. He had been connected more or less closely with the institution since the outset of his professional life, and he was convinced that since carbolic acid had come to be used in the treatment of the surgical cases much good had been done. He had no theory and no prejudice whatever regarding carbolic acid, and only desired to discover the principle on which its action depended, and to learn the truth regarding its value; and he could certainly assert that its employment in the management of compound fractures had been followed by the best results. He would have great pleasure in showing Sir James Simpson cases at present in the wards of the Glasgow Infirmary which he believed it would have been utterly impossible to save from amputation by any method of treatment known to him before he began to use carbolic acid dressings. As to the mortality after amputation, he was aware of the figures on which Sir James Simpson's assertion regarding Glasgow Infirmary was founded, but he would remind his audience how extremely fallacious statistics were unless very carefully collected, and that without any eye to prove a position and without ample explanations. Without entering into so wide a question, he would content himself with remarking, that admitting—which he was by no means prepared to do—that the mortality after amputation had been augmented in Glasgow since carbolic acid dressings had been introduced, it was possible that too much was expected of such applications, and that limbs were tried to be saved by the use of carbolic acid which otherwise would have been amputated early (and so probably saved), till it was too late for successful operation. Some remarks had been made by Sir James Simpson with regard to a series of fifty amputations in private practice, followed by only one death. Unfortunately the operator had lost his notes, and only spoke from a vague memory; but he (Dr. Macleod) would have the honour of recording in the Surgical Section that day the same results from fifty amputations at the ankle (many of them performed in the Glasgow Infirmary), and of which the notes were not lost. The one set might go to balance the other. As he was speaking, he might add a remark or two which had occurred to him while listening to the very able paper of Captain Galton. During the Crimean War, he (Dr. Macleod) had ample experience of the use of both huts and tents in the treatment of sick and wounded, and he claimed having first suggested to the Government the construction, and submitted to them the plans, of such wooden hospitals as had proved such a success on the Dardanelles. Nothing could be more perfect than the adaptability of such temporary structures to the use of an army. When any complication arose, such as secondary hæmorrhage, purulent infection, gangrene, &c., the removal of the patient into tents was always followed by the best results; but to be healthy, both huts and tents had to be frequently moved, as the very ground on which they were erected became impregnated with deleterious emanations. He was much delighted to hear that Sir James Simpson had now come to the same conclusion as himself regarding the size and proper site for hospitals, as many years ago he had read a paper at the Social Science meeting at Glasgow, in which he advocated small establishments in the country to which patients might be sent for operation, and at that time also this question of the difference of mortality in town and country practice was stated by him. Small hospitals scattered throughout a city might provide for the immediate wants of the injured, and so avoid the great danger of transport. A great deal had been said about the internal arrangements of hospitals, but he would plead for more attention to their external surroundings. He had always thought that a fundamental error in the establishment of hospitals was placing them in cities and among many buildings. The larger and older a hospital became, the worse was it adapted for its purpose. He hoped the time would come when small buildings placed among fields and gardens, and having all the aids to recovery which amusements, flowers, and music could contribute, would be the type of our hospitals, and not the present huge piles of courts and towers crowded into the heart of our great manufacturing centres.

APPENDIX.

VENTILATING FIREPLACES.

There are few details of domestic architecture of greater importance in this country than our fireplaces, since as a rule we are dependent on them for comfort during nearly three-fourths of the year. Now, the design of a chimney fire being simply to warm a room, it is necessary first of all to contrive matters so that the room shall be actually warmed; secondly, that it shall be warmed with the smallest expense of fuel possible; and, thirdly, that in warming it the air of the room be preserved perfectly pure and fit for respiration, and free from smoke and all disagreeable smells.

In order to take measures with certainty for warming a room by means of an open chimney fire, it will be necessary to consider *how* or in *what manner* such a fire communicates heat to a room.

In a room warmed by an ordinary fireplace the heat is obtained from the direct radiation into the room of the heat from the incandescent fire, and from the reflected heat from the sides and back of the grate. Nearly seven-eighths of the heat generated by the coal passes with the smoke up the chimney, and carries with it out of the room a large quantity of air, amounting, in even moderate-sized rooms, when the chimney is heated, to as much as from 14,000 cubic feet to 20,000 cubic feet in an hour.

This air must be drawn into the room from somewhere, and unless some arrangement is made for supplying the room with warmed fresh air, cold air finds its way into the room through the chinks of the windows and doors, or wherever it can get in most easily, and thus the temperature at the end of the room furthest from the fire is kept low, the occupants are subjected to draughts, and, if there are two fireplaces in the same room, one of which is not lighted, the air is even frequently drawn down the vacant chimney.

It is essential to health that the air of a room should be renewed, and the oppressive feelings consequent upon the use of close stoves, as in Germany, or hot-water pipes, as contrasted with open fireplaces, arise from the want of a sufficient supply of fresh air.

The experiments made by the Barrack and Hospital Improvement Committee, presided over by the late Lord Herbert, showed that, for a room occupied by several persons to be even moderately ventilated, it was necessary that the quantity of air renewed should amount to at least 1,000 cubic feet per occupant per hour, and they laid down the rule that, assuming each occupant to have 600 cubic feet of space, the air of the room should be completely renewed twice in an hour.

General Morin, the head of the Conservatoire des Arts et Métiers, in Paris, who more than any man has made ventilation his study, has laid down that the air of an ordinary sitting-room should be renewed five times in an hour.

The quantity of air theoretically necessary must depend

upon the number of occupants of a room, but the power of the chimney as a ventilating agent is a fixed quantity, and the number of occupants vary: hence the size of the fireplace and chimney must be fixed with reference to the probable normal use of the room.

In a room furnished with an ordinary open fireplace, with closed doors and windows, the circulation of air proceeds as follows:—

The air is drawn along the floor towards the grate, it is then warmed by the radiating heat of the fire, and part is carried up the chimney with the smoke, whilst the remainder flows upwards near the chimney-breast towards the ceiling. It passes along the ceiling, and, as it cools in its progress towards the opposite wall, descends to the floor, to be again drawn towards the fireplace. It follows from this that the best position in which to deliver the fresh warm air required to take the place of that which has passed up the chimney, is at some convenient point in the chimney-breast, between the chimney-piece and the top of the room, for the air thus falls, consequently, into the current, and mixes with the air of the room without perceptible disturbance.

The ventilating fireplace was designed with the object of obviating the above-named objections to the common fireplace, and of providing such adequate means of ventilating the soldiers' rooms in cold weather when the windows are shut as would not be liable to be deranged.

The limit to which the heat from the fire can be so utilized will be the point at which it cools down the chimney, so as to check the draught and combustion of the fuel.

With respect to the application of the grate to existing buildings, the recess in which an ordinary fire-grate would be fixed forms the chamber in which the air is warmed. In order to afford facilities for the occasional cleansing of this chamber, and those parts of the air-channels connected with it, the front of the stove is secured by screws, so that it can be easily removed, thus rendering the air-chambers accessible.

The stove was designed with the object of being applied to existing chimney openings. In so applying it, the air-chamber is to be left as large as possible, thoroughly cleansed from old soot, and rendered clean with cement, and lime-whited. Should the fireplace be deeper than 1 ft. 6 in., which is the depth required for the curved iron smoke-flue, then a lining of brickwork is to be built up at the back, to reduce it to that dimension. The chimney-bars, if too high, must be lowered to suit the height of the stove, or to a height above the hearth of 3 ft. 3 in.; they must also be straightened, to receive the covering of the air-chambers. These coverings should be of 3 in. York or other flagging, cut out to receive the curved iron smoke-flue, and also to form the bottom of the warm-air flue in the chimney-breast. In new buildings the air-chambers may be rectangular; they must be 4 in. narrower than the extreme dimensions of the moulded frame of the stove, so as to give a margin of 2 in. in width all round for a bedding of hair mortar.

Mr. Edward Deane, of 1, Arthur Street East, E.C., has recently undertaken to provide and fix these ventilating fire-places; but they are not patented. The stove is of the best cast-iron, and consists of three pieces, properly connected by screws. The first piece forms the moulded projecting frame; the second, the body of the grate; and the third, the nozzle or connexion with the smoke-flue, the bottom flange of which is bolted to the back of the grate. The stoves are of three sizes:—The largest has an opening for fire of 1 ft. 9 in. wide, and was intended for rooms containing from 8,000 to 12,000 cubic feet; it weighs about 3 cwt. 1 qr. 10 lbs. The second, or medium size, has an opening for fire 1 ft. 5 in. wide, and was intended for rooms containing from 3,600 to 8,400 cubic feet; it weighs about 2 cwt. 3 qrs. 5 lbs. The third, or smallest size, has an opening for fire 1 ft. 3 in. wide, and was intended for rooms containing 3,600 cubic feet and under; it weighs about 2 cwt. 2 qrs.

The figures appended show an elevation, section, and plan of the second or medium-size stove, the extreme dimensions of which are 40 inches wide by 42 inches high; the projecting moulded frame enables the stove to be applied to any existing chimney-opening.

The fireplace has a lining of fire-lumps in five pieces; two sides, one back-piece, and two bottom pieces, moulded to the form shown in the woodcut. The bottom is partly solid, being made of two fire-lumps placed one on each side, and supporting an intermediate cast-iron fire-grating, which occupies about one-third of the bottom of the grate; by this means, whilst the draught is checked and the consumption of fuel reduced, a sufficient supply of air for combustion at the bottom to secure a cheerful fire is obtained. A clear space, half an inch deep, is formed between the back lump and iron back to receive a supply of air through the ash-pit under the grate, which passes through a slit in the fire-lump immediately above the fire. The air thus brought into contact with the heated coal is received at a high temperature, in consequence of passing through the heated fire-lump, and is forced into contact with the gases from the coal by means of the piece of fire-lump which projects over the fire at the back of the grate, and thus a more perfect combustion of the smoke is effected than with an ordinary grate; in fact, with care, almost perfect combustion of the fuel, and consequent utilization of the heat, can be obtained.

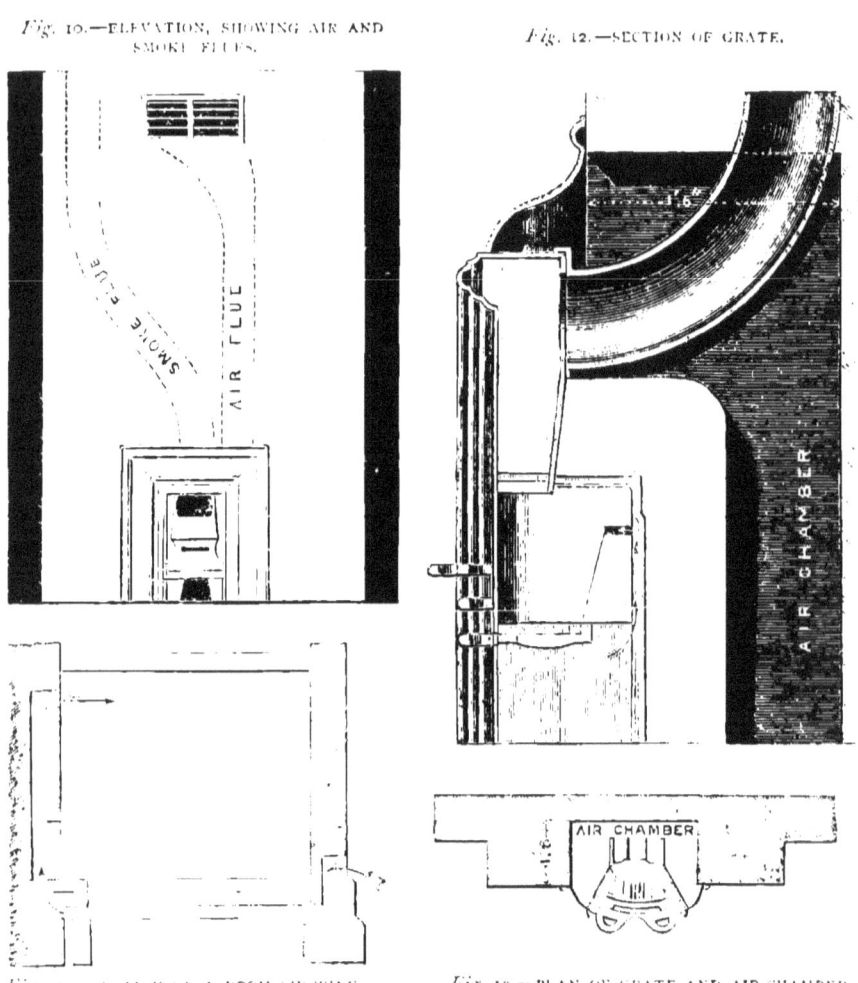

Fig. 10.—ELEVATION, SHOWING AIR AND SMOKE FLUES.

Fig. 12.—SECTION OF GRATE.

Fig. 11.—SECTION OF A ROOM SHOWING AIR-FLUE AND FLUE.

Fig. 13.—PLAN OF GRATE AND AIR-CHAMBER.

The flame, heated gases from combustion, and such small amount of smoke as exists, are compelled, by the form of the back of the grate and the iron part of the smoke-flue, to impinge upon a large heating surface, so as to subtract as much heat as possible out of them before they pass into the chimney, and the heat thus extracted is employed to warm air taken directly from the outer air. The air is warmed by the iron back of the stove and smoke-flue, upon both of which broad flanges are cast so as to obtain a large surface of metal to give off the heat. This giving-off surface (amounting in the case of No. 1 grate to 13·5 square feet) is sufficient to prevent the fire in the grate from ever rendering the back so hot as to burn the air it is employed to heat. The fresh air, after it has been warmed, is passed into the room near the ceiling by the flue shown in the woodcut.

The flue which has been adopted for barracks is carried up by the side of the smoke-flue in the chimney-breast. It will be seen from the illustration that there is in the air-chamber of No. 1 grate a heating surface for warming the air of about 13·5 square feet.

The mode of admitting external air into this chamber must depend upon the locality of the fireplace. If the fireplace be built in an external wall, the opening for fresh air can be made in the back; but if in an internal wall, it will be necessary to construct a channel from the outside, either between the flooring of the room and the ceiling joists of the room below (if there be independent ceiling joists), or between the floor boards and the plaster ceiling, in the spaces between the joists, or by a tube or hollow beam carried below the ceiling of the room altogether. In any case, however, these horizontal ducts should contain one superficial inch of sectional area for every 100 cubic feet of room space; the grating covering the opening to the outer air need not be larger in total area than the flue, so that the clear area through the grating would only be about half that of the flue. If the shafts are of considerable length, the sectional area should be rather more; but if there be a direct communication with the outer air, the sectional area should be rather less than that recommended.

There is one point connected with the flue which must be carefully attended to—viz. the fresh air should be taken from places where impurities cannot affect it, and the flue must be so arranged and constructed as to afford easy means of being periodically thoroughly examined and cleaned. In barracks the rule is that such cleansing should take place at least once a year.

The area of the grate of No. 1 stove is 84 square inches, of which 58 are solid, and 26 afford space in the centre for the passing of air. The front is open, and air is passed on to the coal from the back in the manner already described. The grate will contain about 18 to 20 lbs. of coal; when the fire is maintained for from twelve to fifteen hours, a total consumption of about 2·5 lbs. per hour, or 40 lbs. for sixteen hours, will suffice to maintain a good fire. For soldiers' rooms the daily allowance in winter with No. 1 grate is nearly 46 lbs. per diem; but this is more than a careful economy would require.

In new buildings it would be possible, and indeed desirable, to extend this heating surface considerably by carrying up the smoke-flue inside the warm-air flue. This plan has been adopted in the fireplaces for the wards of the Herbert Hospital, where the fireplace is in the centre of the ward, and the chimney consequently passes under the floor, and is placed in the centre of the flue which brings in the fresh air to be warmed by the fireplace: by this means a heating surface for the fresh air, of above 36 square feet additional to that of each fireplace, has been obtained.

APPENDIX. 89

The annexed woodcut shows these fireplaces.

Fig. 14.

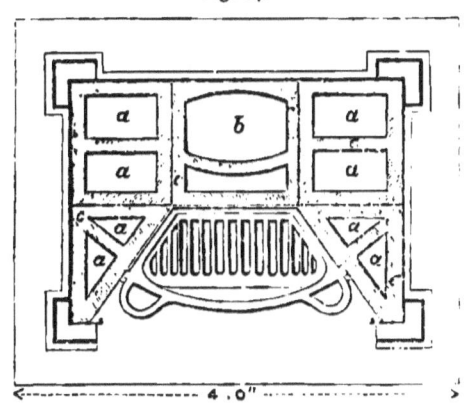

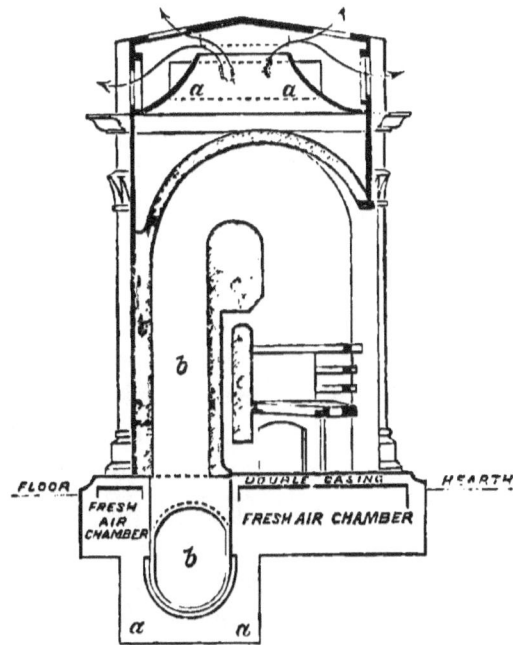

a.a. FRESH AIR FLUES.
b.b. SMOKE FLUE
c.c. FIRE CLAY

The fire stands in an iron cradle fitted to the fire-clay back and sides, and a current of air is brought through the fire-clay at the back, where it becomes heated, on to the top of the fire to assist the combustion, and thus prevent smoke. The top of the stove is coved inside, to lead the smoke easily into the chimney. The main body of the stove is a mass of fire-clay, with flues cast in it, up which the fresh air passes from the horizontal air-flue already mentioned, in which the chimney-flue is laid. Thus all the parts of the stove employed to warm the fresh air with which the fire has direct contact, are of fire-clay.

The area of the horizontal chimney-flue in the Herbert Hospital fireplaces is about 110 square inches. The horizontal chimney-flue terminates in a vertical flue in the side wall, which should be rather larger in area than the horizontal flue. This vertical flue is carried in the upper floors to a height of double the length of the horizontal flue, and is carried down to the basement, where it can be swept. The horizontal flue is swept by pushing a brush along it to force the soot into the vertical flue. There is placed a spare flue by the side of the vertical flue, terminating in a fireplace in the basement, which enables the vertical flue to be warmed, so as either to make it draw when the fire is first lighted, or to enable a current to be maintained for ventilating purposes through the fireplace when the fire is not lighted. The ward floor should be so arranged as to enable the air-flue to be easily and thoroughly cleaned periodically.

The principle of these arrangements for utilizing to some extent the heat in the chimney has been adopted for barracks in the case of grates for married soldiers; these would be useful as cottage grates. These latter grates have been made for the War Department by Messrs. Benham, of

Wigmore Street, London. They have a small oven, and an open fire; warmed air is introduced into the room by means of an iron flue carried up from the fire-brick lining of the stove inside the chimney, and introduced into the room near the ceiling through a louvred opening: by this means the heat of the smoke is utilized. This description of grate

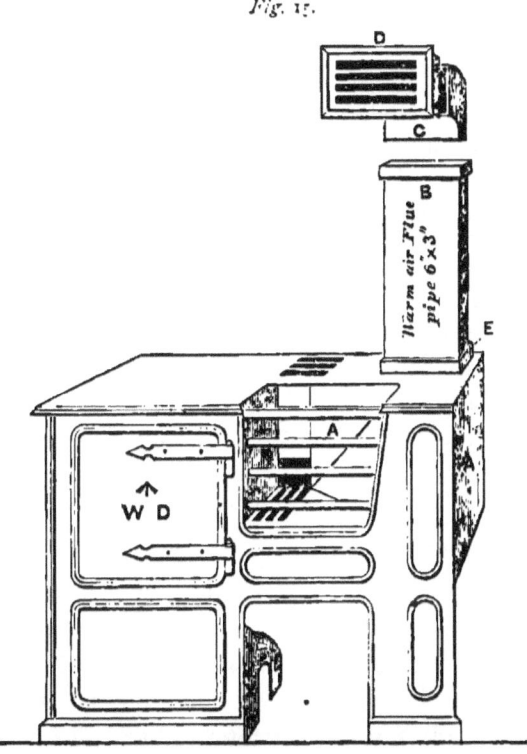

Fig. 15.

A. Fire-lump with warm-air flue through back.
B. Warm-air pipe to fit into socket on hob, in lengths of 1 ft. 3 in. each.
C. Bend to fit socket of the above pipe.
D. Mouth piece with Louvre front to fit on bend.
 No. 1 of these 6 in. long supplied with each range.
 Increased heating surface for the hot air is provided by means of a grating inside the socket at E.

was devised for the purpose of combining a power of cooking for a cottage with great compulsory economy of fuel (see fig. 15). It must, however, always be observed that in proportion as the heat is removed from the chimney, so is the draught, *i.e.* the effect of the chimney as a pumping engine to remove the air, diminished, and the combustion of the fuel to some extent checked.

Numerous experiments have been made on the fireplace, and it will suffice to recapitulate some of those made by independent persons.

Experiments made upon the quantity of air supplied and the temperature maintained show that the air is generally admitted into the rooms at a temperature of from 20 deg. to 30 deg. Fahr. above that of the outer air. The design of the grate was intended to preclude the possibility of such a temperature as would in any way injure the air introduced; and the experiments made by Dr. Parkes in a hospital ward at Chatham, in April 1864, illustrate the hygrometric effect with the grate in use. The greatest difference between the dry and wet bulbs in the ward was:—On the 17th, 8·5 deg.; on the 18th, 6·0 deg.; on the 19th. 5·5 deg.; on the 20th, 6·5 deg.; on the 21st, 5·0 deg. On examining the record of the dry and wet bulbs during these days, no evidence can be seen at any time of any unusual or improper dryness of the atmosphere. The difference between the two bulbs was certainly always greater in the ward, but it was not material. The temperature of the rooms was invariably found to be so equable that when the grate was in full action, and the windows and other means of ventilation closed, thermometers placed in different parts of the room, near the ceiling and floor, in corners furthest from the fire, and on the side nearest to it, but sheltered from the radiating effect of the fire, did not vary more than about 1 deg. Fahr. The variation of temperature in a room warmed by a fire, by radiation, without the action of warmed

APPENDIX. 93

air, will be found to be from 4 deg. to 6 deg. Fahr., and sometimes even much more in cold weather.

The amount of air delivered through the fresh air shaft varies somewhat with the direction of the wind. The inlet shaft no doubt acts best when the windows, doors, and other inlets are closed, as it then becomes the sole inlet for the room; a velocity of as much as nine or ten feet per second has been observed in the inlet, but this is exceptional.

In the ventilation of barrack-rooms or hospitals, it was not intended that the fresh air warmed by the grate should be the whole supply of fresh air, nor that the chimney should be the sole means employed for the removal of the air to be extracted. In ordinary houses, however, the grate, if adopted, might be used in such a manner as to perform the whole functions of ventilation. In this case it is of course necessary to remember that the ventilating power is a fixed quantity, and that in originally settling the size of grate for a particular room it will be necessary to bear in mind the general object for which the room is to be employed and the number of persons by whom it is required to be occupied with efficient ventilation, because all experiments show that no room can be considered even tolerably ventilated unless at least 1,000 cubic feet of air per occupant are renewed per hour; consequently a room 20 feet long by 15 feet wide and 10 feet high (*i.e.* with 3,000 cubic feet of space), with three people in it, would not require the air to be changed much more than once an hour; whilst, if occupied by twelve or fourteen people, it would require change five times an hour. Of course if the normal use of the room was for three people it would not be worth while to provide for the extra number by which it might be occupied, as their wants in such a temporary case could be met by open windows.

General Morin, with the object of utilizing the grate as the sole means of ventilation for a room, lays down the principle that the whole of the air shall be renewed five times in the hour. To perform this effectually, it is necessary that the area of the top of the chimney shall afford about one square inch of area for every 100 cubic feet of content of the room, and that the area of the fresh air inlet should afford about 14 square inches for every 100 cubic feet of content of the room. But on an average this quantity of air is more than is necessary. The Barrack and Hospital Improvement Committee's proposal would resolve itself into this—viz. that the air in barrack-rooms should be completely changed about twice in an hour, inasmuch as they required a cubic space of 600 cubic feet per man, and for all ordinary purposes this would probably suffice; as, however, this proposal was based on a limited number of occupants, with a more crowded room the amount must be increased.

General Morin made numerous experiments on this form of ventilation in 1864-5-6, with fireplaces constructed in the form in use for barracks, and with others in which the chimney was utilized for warming the air. The details of the experiments are published in the "Annales du Conservatoire des Arts et Métiers" for the years in question.

It will here suffice to state that whilst with an ordinary fireplace the heat which is utilized in a room is only $\frac{1}{8}$ of the heat given off by the coal, or ·125, in these experiments the heat utilized in the room was ·355 of the heat given off by the coal, or $\frac{1}{3}$; therefore, to produce the same degree of warmth in a room, this grate requires little more than one-third of the quantity of coal required by an ordinary grate. The ventilation was effected by passing a volume of air through the room in one hour equal to five times the cubic contents of the room. An equable temperature was maintained during the experiment. There was no perceptible draught, and although the doors fitted badly, scarcely any air was drawn in through the crevices.

In conclusion, the merits which are claimed for this fireplace are :—

1. That it ventilates the room.
2. That it maintains an equable temperature in all parts of the room, and prevents all draughts.
3. That the heat from radiation is thrown into the room better than from other grates.
4. That the fire-brick lining prevents the fire from going out, even when left untouched for a long time, and prevents the rapid changes of temperature which occur in rooms in cold weather from that cause.
5. That it economises fuel partly by making use of the spare heat, which otherwise would all pass up the chimney, and partly by ensuring by its construction a more complete combustion, and thereby diminishing smoke.
6. That it prevents smoky chimneys by the ample supply of warmed air to the room, and by the draught created in the neck of the chimney.

THE END.

LONDON:
R. CLAY, SONS, AND TAYLOR, PRINTERS,
BREAD STREET HILL.

BEDFORD STREET, COVENT GARDEN, LONDON,
March, 1879.

MACMILLAN & CO.'S MEDICAL CATALOGUE.

WORKS in PHYSIOLOGY, ANATOMY, ZOOLOGY, BOTANY, CHEMISTRY, PHYSICS, MIDWIFERY, MATERIA MEDICA, *and other Professional Subjects.*

ALLBUTT (T. C.)—ON THE USE OF THE OPHTHALMOSCOPE in Diseases of the Nervous System and of the Kidneys; also in certain other General Disorders. By THOMAS CLIFFORD ALLBUTT, M.A., M.D., Cantab., Physician to the Leeds General Infirmary, Lecturer on Practical Medicine, &c., &c. 8vo. 15s.

ANDERSON.—Works by DR. McCALL ANDERSON, Professor of Clinical Medicine in the University of Glasgow, and Physician to the Western Infirmary and to the Wards for Skin Diseases.
ON THE TREATMENT OF DISEASES OF THE SKIN; with an Analysis of Eleven Thousand Consecutive Cases. Crown 8vo. 5s.
LECTURES ON CLINICAL MEDICINE. With Illustrations. 8vo. 10s. 6d.
ON THE CURABILITY OF ATTACKS OF TUBERCULAR PERITONITIS AND ACUTE PHTHISIS (Galloping Consumption). Crown 8vo. 2s. 6d.

ANSTIE.—ON THE USE OF WINES IN HEALTH AND DISEASE. By F. E. ANSTIE, M.D., F.R.S., late Physician to Westminster Hospital, and Editor of *The Practitioner*. Crown 8vo. 2s.

BALFOUR.—ELASMOBRANCH FISHES; a Monograph on the Development of. By F. M. BALFOUR, M.A., Fellow and Lecturer of Trinity College, Cambridge. With Plates. 8vo. 21s.

BARWELL.—ON CURVATURES OF THE SPINE: their Causes and treatment. By RICHARD BARWELL, F.R.C.S., Surgeon and late Lecturer on Anatomy at the Charing Cross Hospital. Third Edition, with additional Illustrations. Crown 8vo. 5s.

BASTIAN.—Works by H. CHARLTON BASTIAN, M.D., F.R.S., Professor of Pathological Anatomy in University College, London, &c.:—
THE BEGINNINGS OF LIFE: Being some Account of the Nature, Modes of Origin, and Transformations of Lower Organisms. In Two Volumes. With upwards of 100 Illustrations. Crown 8vo. 28s.
EVOLUTION AND THE ORIGIN OF LIFE. Crown 8vo. 6s. 6d.
ON PARALYSIS FROM BRAIN DISEASE IN ITS COMMON FORMS. Illustrated. Crown 8vo. 10s. 6d.
"It would be a good thing if all such lectures were as clear, as systematic, and as interesting. . . . . It is of interest not only to students but to all who make nervous diseases a study."—*Journal of Mental Science*.

BUCKNILL.—HABITUAL DRUNKENNESS AND INSANE DRUNKARDS. By J. C. BUCKNILL, M.D. Lond., F.R.S., F.R.C.P., late Lord Chancellor's Visitor of Lunatics. Crown 8vo. 2s. 6d.

CARTER.—Works by R. BRUDENELL CARTER, F.R.C.S., Ophthalmic Surgeon to St. George's Hospital, &c.
A PRACTICAL TREATISE ON DISEASES OF THE EYE. With Illustrations. 8vo. 16s.
"No one will read Mr. Carter's book without having both his special and general knowledge increased."—*Lancet*.
ON DEFECTS OF VISION WHICH ARE REMEDIABLE BY OPTICAL APPLIANCES. Lectures at the Royal College of Surgeons. With numerous Illustrations. 8vo. 6s.

3,000.3.79.

CHRISTIE.—CHOLERA EPIDEMICS IN EAST AFRICA. An Account of the several Diffusions of the Disease in that country from 1821 till 1872, with an Outline of the Geography, Ethnology, and Trade Connections of the Regions through which the Epidemics passed. By J. CHRISTIE, M.D., late Physician to H.H. the Sultan of Zanzibar. With Maps. 8vo. 15s.

COOKE (JOSIAH P., Jun.).—FIRST PRINCIPLES OF CHEMICAL PHILOSOPHY. By JOSIAH P. COOKE, Jun., Ervine Professor of Chemistry and Mineralogy in Harvard College. Third Edition, revised and corrected. Crown 8vo. 12s.

CREIGHTON. — CONTRIBUTIONS TO THE PHYSIOLOGY AND PATHOLOGY OF THE BREAST AND ITS LYMPHATIC GLANDS. By CHARLES CREIGHTON, M.D., Demonstrator of Anatomy in the University of Cambridge. With Illustrations. 8vo. 9s.

"It is impossible not to see at once that the work is deserving of all praise, both from the originality and from the care which has been bestowed upon it."—*Practitioner.*

FLOWER (W. H.).—AN INTRODUCTION TO THE OSTEOLOGY OF THE MAMMALIA. Being the substance of the Course of Lectures delivered at the Royal College of Surgeons of England in 1870. By W. H. FLOWER, F.R.S., F.R.C.S., Hunterian Professor of Comparative Anatomy and Physiology. With numerous Illustrations. Second Edition, revised and enlarged. Crown 8vo. 10s. 6d.

FOSTER.—Works by MICHAEL FOSTER, M.D., F.R.S. :—

A TEXT BOOK OF PHYSIOLOGY, for the use of Medical Students and others. Second Edition, revised and enlarged, with additional Plates and Illustrations. 8vo. 21s.

"Dr. Foster has combined in this work the conflicting desiderata in all text-books—comprehensiveness, brevity, and clearness. After a careful perusal of the whole work we can confidently recommend it, both to the student and the practitioner as being one of the best text-books on physiology extant."—*Lancet.*

A PRIMER OF PHYSIOLOGY. Illustrated. 18mo. 1s.

FOSTER and LANGLEY.—AN ELEMENTARY COURSE OF PRACTICAL PHYSIOLOGY. By MICHAEL FOSTER, M.D., F.R.S., assisted by J. N. LANGLEY, B.A. Third Edition, enlarged. Crown 8vo. 6s.

"Equipped with a text-book such as this .... the beginner cannot fail to acquire a real, though of course elementary, knowledge of the leading facts and principles of Physiology."—*Academy.*

FOSTER and BALFOUR.—ELEMENTS OF EMBRYOLOGY. By MICHAEL FOSTER, M.D., F.R.S., and F. M. BALFOUR, M.A., Fellow of Trinity College, Cambridge. With numerous Illustrations. Part I. Crown 8vo. 7s. 6d.

"Both text and illustrations are alike remarkable for their clearness and freedom from error, indicating the immense amount of labour and care expended in the production of this most valuable addition to scientific literature."—*Medical Press and Circular.*

FOTHERGILL. — Works by J. MILNER FOTHERGILL, M.D., M.R.C.P., Assistant Physician to the Victoria Park Chest Hospital, and to the West London Hospital :—

THE PRACTITIONER'S HANDBOOK OF TREATMENT : or, THE PRINCIPLES OF RATIONAL THERAPEUTICS. 8vo. 14s.

"We have every reason to thank the author for a practical and suggestive work."—*Lancet.*

THE ANTAGONISM OF THERAPEUTIC AGENTS, AND WHAT IT TEACHES. The Essay to which was awarded the Fothergillian Gold Medal of the Medical Society of London for 1878. Crown 8vo. 6s.

FOX.—Works by WILSON FOX, M.D., Lond., F.R.C.P., F.R.S., Holme Professor of Clinical Medicine, University College, London, Physician Extraordinary to her Majesty the Queen, &c. :—

DISEASES OF THE STOMACH: being a new and revised Edition of "THE DIAGNOSIS AND TREATMENT OF THE VARIETIES OF DYSPEPSIA." 8vo. 8s. 6d.

ON THE ARTIFICIAL PRODUCTION OF TUBERCLE IN THE LOWER ANIMALS. With Coloured Plates. 4to. 5s. 6d.

ON THE TREATMENT OF HYPERPYREXIA, as Illustrated in Acute Articular Rheumatism by means of the External Application of Cold. 8vo. 2s. 6d.

GALTON (D.).—AN ADDRESS ON THE GENERAL PRINCIPLES WHICH SHOULD BE OBSERVED IN THE CONSTRUCTION OF HOSPITALS. By DOUGLAS GALTON, C.B., F.R.S. Crown 8vo. 3s. 6d.

GEGENBAUR.—ELEMENTS OF COMPARATIVE ANATOMY. By CARL GEGENBAUR, Professor of Anatomy and Director of the Anatomical Institute, Heidelberg. A translation by F. JEFFREY BELL, B.A., revised, with Preface by E. RAY LANKESTER, M.A., F.R.S., Professor of Zoology and Comparative Anatomy in University College, London. With numerous Illustrations. Medium 8vo. 21s.

GRIFFITHS.—LESSONS ON PRESCRIPTIONS AND THE ART OF PRESCRIBING. By W. HANSEL GRIFFITHS, Ph.D., L.R.C.P.E. New Edition. 18mo. 3s. 6d.

"We recommend it to all students and junior members of the profession who desire to understand the art of prescribing."—*Medical Press.*

HANBURY.—SCIENCE PAPERS, chiefly Pharmacological and Botanical. By DANIEL HANBURY, F.R.S. Edited with Memoir by JOSEPH INCE, F.L.S., F.C.S. 8vo. 14s.

HOOD (Wharton.).—ON BONE-SETTING (so-called), and its Relation to the Treatment of Joints Crippled by Injury, Rheumatism, Inflammation, &c., &c. By WHARTON P. HOOD, M.D., M.R.C.S. Crown 8vo. Illustrated. 4s. 6d.

"Dr. Hood's book is full of instruction, and should be read by all surgeons."—*Medical Times.*

HOOKER (Dr.).—THE STUDENT'S FLORA OF THE BRITISH ISLANDS. By Sir J. D. HOOKER, K.C.S.I., C.B., M.D., D.C.L., President of the Royal Society. Second Edition, revised and corrected. Globe 8vo. 10s. 6d.

HUMPHRY.—Works by G. M. HUMPHRY, M.D., F.R.S., Professor of Anatomy in the University of Cambridge, and Honorary Fellow of Downing College :—

THE HUMAN SKELETON (including the Joints). With 260 Illustrations drawn from Nature. Medium 8vo. 28s.

OBSERVATIONS IN MYOLOGY. Illustrated. 8vo. 6s.

THE HUMAN FOOT AND HAND. Illustrated. Fcap. 8vo. 4s. 6d.

HUXLEY and MARTIN.—A COURSE OF PRACTICAL INSTRUCTION IN ELEMENTARY BIOLOGY. By T. H. HUXLEY, LL.D. Sec. R.S., assisted by H. N. MARTIN, M.B., D.Sc. New Edition, revised. Crown 8vo. 6s.

"To intending medical students this book will prove of great value."—*Lancet.*

HUXLEY (Professor).—LESSONS IN ELEMENTARY PHYSIOLOGY. By T. H. HUXLEY, LL.D., F.R.S. With numerous Illustrations. New Edition. Fcap. 8vo. 4s. 6d.

KEETLEY.—THE STUDENT'S GUIDE TO THE MEDICAL
PROFESSION. By C. B. KEETLEY, F.R.C S., Assistant Surgeon to the West
London Hospital. With a Chapter for Women Students. By Mrs. GARRETT
ANDERSON. Crown 8vo. 2s. 6d.

KÜHNE.—ON THE PHOTOCHEMISTRY OF THE RETINA
AND ON VISUAL PURPLE. Translated from the German of Dr. KÜHNE,
and Edited, with Notes, by MICHAEL FOSTER, M.D., F.R.S. 8vo. 3s. 6d.

LANKESTER.—COMPARATIVE LONGEVITY IN MAN AND
THE LOWER ANIMALS. By E. RAY LANKESTER B.A. Crown 8vo.
4s. 6d.

LEISHMAN.—A SYSTEM OF MIDWIFERY, including the
Diseases of Pregnancy and the Puerperal State. By WILLIAM LEISHMAN.
M.D., Regius Professor of Midwifery in the University of Glasgow: Physician
to the University Lying-in Hospital: Fellow and late Vice-President of the
Obstetrical Society of London, &c., &c. 8vo. Illustrated. Second and Cheaper
Edition. 21s.

MACLAGAN. — THE GERM THEORY APPLIED TO THE
EXPLANATION OF THE PHENOMENA OF DISEASE. By T. MACLAGAN,
M.D. 8vo. 10s. 6d.
"We think it well that such a book as this should be written. It places before
the reader in clear and unmistakable language what is meant by the germ theory of
disease."—*Lancet.*

MACNAMARA.—Works by C. MACNAMARA, F.C.U., Surgeon
to Westminster Hospital :—

A HISTORY OF ASIATIC CHOLERA. Crown 8vo. 10s. 6d.
"A very valuable contribution to medical literature, and well worthy of the place
which it is sure to assume as the standard work on the subject. —*Medical Examiner.*

DISEASES OF BONE.—CLINICAL LECTURES. Crown 8vo. 5s.

MACPHERSON.—Works by JOHN MACPHERSON, M.D. :—
THE BATHS AND WELLS OF EUROPE: their Action and Uses. With
Notices of Climatic Resorts and Diet Cures. With a Map. New Edition,
revised and enlarged. Extra fcap. 8vo. 6s. 6d.

OUR BATHS AND WELLS: The Mineral Waters of the British Islands. With
a List of Sea-bathing Places. Extra fcap. 8vo. 3s. 6d.

MANSFIELD (C. B.).—A THEORY OF SALTS. A Treatise on
the Constitution of Bipolar (two-membered) Chemical Compounds. By the
late CHARLES BLACHFORD MANSFIELD. Crown 8vo. 14s.

MAUDSLEY.—Works by HENRY MAUDSLEY, M.D., Professor of
Medical Jurisprudence in University College, London :—

BODY AND MIND: An Inquiry into their Connection and Mutual Influence,
specially in reference to Mental Disorders: being the Gulstonian Lectures
for 1870. Delivered before the Royal College of Physicians. New Edition,
with Psychological Essays added. Crown 8vo. 6s. 6d.

THE PHYSIOLOGY OF MIND. Being the First Part of a Third Edition,
revised, enlarged, and in great part re-written, of "The Physiology and Pathology of Mind." Crown 8vo. 10s. 6d.

THE PATHOLOGY OF MIND. [*In the Press.*

MIALL.--STUDIES IN COMPARATIVE ANATOMY.
No. I.—The Skull of the Crocodile. By L. C. MIALL, Professor of Biology
in the Yorkshire College of Science. 8vo. 2s 6d.
No II.—The Anatomy of the Indian Elephant. By L. C. MIALL and F. GREEN-
WOOD, Curator of the Leeds School of Medicine. Illustrated. 8vo. 5s.

MIVART (St. George).—Works by St. George Mivart, F.R.S., &c., Lecturer in Comparative Anatomy at St. Mary's Hospital :—

ON THE GENESIS OF SPECIES. Second Edition, to which notes have been added in reference and reply to Darwin's " Descent of Man." With numerous Illustrations. Crown 8vo. 9s.

LESSONS IN ELEMENTARY ANATOMY. With upwards of 400 Illustrations, New Edition. Fcap. 8vo. 6s. 6d.

"It may be questioned whether any other work on anatomy contains in like compass so proportionately great a mass of information."—*Lancet.*

M'KENDRICK.—OUTLINES OF PHYSIOLOGY IN ITS RELATIONS TO MAN. By John Gray M'Kendrick, M.D., F.R.S.E., Professor of the Institute of Medicine and Physiology in the University of Glasgow. Illustrated. Crown 8vo. 12s. 6d.

MUIR.—PRACTICAL CHEMISTRY FOR MEDICAL STUDENTS. Specially arranged for the first M. B. Course. By M. M. Pattison Muir, F.R.S.E., Prælector in Chemistry, Caius College, Cambridge. Fcap. 8vo. 1s. 6d.

"This little book will aid the student not only to pass his professional examination in practical Chemistry more easily, but will give him such an insight into the subject as will enable him readily to extend his knowledge of it should time and inclination permit."—*Practitioner.*

OLIVER.—LESSONS IN ELEMENTARY BOTANY. By Daniel Oliver, F.R.S., F.L.S., Professor of Botany in University College, London, and Keeper of the Herbarium and Library of the Royal Gardens, Kew. With nearly 200 Illustrations. New Edition. Fcap. 8vo. 4s. 6d.

PARKER and BETTANY.—THE MORPHOLOGY OF THE SKULL. By W. K. Parker, F.R.S., Hunterian Professor, Royal College of Surgeons, and G. T. Bettany, M.A., B.Sc., Lecturer on Botany in Guy's Hospital Medical School. Crown 8vo. 10s. 6d.

PETTIGREW.—THE PHYSIOLOGY OF THE CIRCULATION IN PLANTS, IN THE LOWER ANIMALS, AND IN MAN. By J. Bell Pettigrew, M.D., F.R.S., etc. Illustrated by 150 Woodcuts. 8vo. 12s.

"A more original, interesting, exhaustive, or comprehensive treatise on the circulation and the circulatory apparatus in plants, animals, and man, has never, we are certain, been offered for the acceptance of the anatomist physiologist or student of medicine."—*Veterinary Journal.*

PIFFARD.—AN ELEMENTARY TREATISE ON DISEASES OF THE SKIN, for the Use of Students and Practitioners. By H. G. Piffard, M.D., Professor of Dermatology in the University of the City of New York, &c. With Illustrations. 8vo. 16s.

RADCLIFFE.—Works by Charles Bland Radcliffe, M.D., F.R.C.P., Physician to the Westminster Hospital, and to the National Hospital for the Paralysed and Epileptic:—

VITAL MOTION AS A MODE OF PHYSICAL MOTION. Crown 8vo. 8s. 6d.

PROTEUS; OR UNITY IN NATURE. Second Edition. 8vo. 7s. 6d.

RANSOME.—ON STETHOMETRY. Chest Examination by a more Exact Method with its Results. With an Appendix on the Chemical and Microscopical Examination of Respired Air. By Arthur Ransome, M.D. With Illustrations. 8vo. 10s. 6d.

"We can recommend his book not only to those who are interested in the graphic method, but to all who are specially concerned in the treatment of diseases of the chest."—*British Medical Journal.*

REYNOLDS (J. R.).—A SYSTEM OF MEDICINE. Edited by J. Russell Reynolds, M.D., F.R.S. London. In 5 Vols. Vols. I. to III., 25s. each; Vol IV., 21s.; Vol. V., 25s.

REYNOLDS (J. R.).—*continued.*
 VOL. I.—Part I. General Diseases, or Affections of the Whole System. Part II. Local Diseases, or Affections of Particular Systems. § I.—Diseases of the Skin.
 VOL. II.—Part II. Local Diseases (continued). § I.—Diseases of the Nervous System. § II.—Diseases of the Digestive System.
 VOL. III.—Part II. Local Diseases (continued). § II.—Diseases of the Digestive System (continued). § III.—Diseases of the Respiratory System.
 VOL. IV.—Diseases of the Heart. Part II. Local Diseases (continued). § IV.—Diseases of the Organs of Circulation.
 VOL. V.—Diseases of the Organs of Circulation.—Diseases of the Vessels.—Diseases of the Blood-Glandular System.—Diseases of the Urinary Organs.—Diseases of the Female Reproductive Organs.—Diseases of the Cutaneous System.
 Also, now publishing in MONTHLY PARTS, Price 5s. each, to be completed in 24 Parts. (Part 1, April 1st, 1879.)

RICHARDSON.—Works by B. W. RICHARDSON, M.D., F.R.S. :—
 DISEASES OF MODERN LIFE. Fifth and Cheaper Edition. Crown 8vo. 6s.
 ON ALCOHOL. New Edition. Crown 8vo. 1s.
 HYGEIA, A CITY OF HEALTH. Crown 8vo. 1s.
 THE FUTURE OF SANITARY SCIENCE. Crown 8vo. 1s.
 TOTAL ABSTINENCE. A course of addresses. Crown 8vo. 3s. 6d.

ROSCOE.—Works by HENRY ROSCOE, F.R.S., Professor of Chemistry in Owens College, Manchester :—
 LESSONS IN ELEMENTARY CHEMISTRY, INORGANIC AND ORGANIC. With numerous Illustrations, and Chromolithographs of the Solar Spectrum and of the Alkalies and Alkaline Earths. New Edition. Fcap. 8vo. 4s. 6d.
 CHEMICAL PROBLEMS, adapted to the above. By Professor T. E. THORPE, M.D., F.R.S.E., with Preface by Professor Roscoe. Fifth Edition, with Key. 18mo. 2s.
 PRIMER OF CHEMISTRY. Illustrated. 18mo. 1s.

ROSCOE and SCHORLEMMER.—A TREATISE ON CHEMISTRY. By Professors ROSCOE and SCHORLEMMER. Vol. I. The Non-Metallic Elements. With Numerous Illustrations and Portrait of Dalton. 8vo. 21s. Vol. II. Metals. Part 1. With numerous Illustrations. 8vo. 21s.

SCHORLEMMER.—A MANUAL OF THE CHEMISTRY OF THE CARBON COMPOUNDS, OR ORGANIC CHEMISTRY. By C. SCHORLEMMER, F.R.S., Lecturer in Organic Chemistry in Owens College, Manchester. 8vo. 14s.

SEATON.—A HANDBOOK OF VACCINATION. By EDWARD C. SEATON, M.D., Medical Inspector to the Privy Council. Extra fcap. 8vo. 8s. 6d.

SEILER.—MICRO-PHOTOGRAPHS IN HISTOLOGY, Normal and Pathological. By CARL SEILER, M.D., in conjunction with J. GIBBONS HUNT, M.D., and J. G. RICHARDSON, M.D. 4to. 31s. 6d.

SPENDER.—THERAPEUTIC MEANS FOR THE RELIEF OF PAIN, Being the Prize Essay for which the Medical Society of London awarded the Fothergillian Gold Medal in 1874. By JOHN KENT SPENDER, M.D. Lond., Surgeon to the Mineral Water Hospital, Bath. 8vo. 8s. 6d.

STEWART (B.).—LESSONS IN ELEMENTARY PHYSICS. By BALFOUR STEWART, F.R.S., Professor of Natural Philosophy in Owens College, Manchester. With Numerous Illustrations and Chromolithograph of the Spectra of the Sun, Stars, and Nebulæ. New Edition. Fcap. 8vo. 4s. 6d.

PRIMER OF PHYSICS. By the same Author. Illustrated. 18mo. 1s.

TUKE.—INSANITY IN ANCIENT AND MODERN LIFE, with Chapters on its Prevention. By D. HACK TUKE, M.D., F.R.C.P. Crown 8vo. 6s.

"This work exhibits deep research in various directions, and teems with allusions and quotations which prove the author to be not only an accomplished psychological physician, but a scholar of no mean order."—*Medical Times.*

WEST.—HOSPITAL ORGANISATION. With special reference to the organisation of Hospitals for Children. By CHARLES WEST, M.D. Founder of, and for twenty-three years Physician to, the Hospital for Sick Children. Crown 8vo. 2s. 6d.

WURTZ.—A HISTORY OF CHEMICAL THEORY from the Age of Lavoisier down to the present time. By AD. WURTZ. Translated by HENRY WATTS, F.R.S. Crown 8vo. 6s.

MANUALS FOR STUDENTS.

THE MORPHOLOGY OF THE SKULL. By W. K. PARKER, F.R.S., Hunterian Professor, Royal College of Surgeons, and G. T. BETTANY, B.Sc., Lecturer on Botany in Guy's Hospital Medical School. Illustrated. Crown 8vo. 10s. 6d.

THE OSTEOLOGY OF THE MAMMALIA: A Series of Lectures by Prof. W. H. FLOWER, F.R.S., F.R.C.S. With numerous Illustrations. New Edition, enlarged. Crown 8vo. 10s. 6d.

THE ELEMENTS OF EMBRYOLOGY. By MICHAEL FOSTER, M.D., F.R.S., and F. M. BALFOUR, M.A. Part I. 7s. 6d.

PRACTICAL PHYSIOLOGY: an Elementary Course of. By Dr. M. FOSTER, assisted by J. LANGLEY. New Edition. Crown 8vo. 6s.

ELEMENTARY BIOLOGY: a Course of Practical Instruction in. By Prof. HUXLEY and H. N. MARTIN. New Edition. Crown 8vo. 6s.

PHYSIOGRAPHY: an Introduction to the Study of Nature. By Prof. HUXLEY, F.R.S. With Coloured Plates and Woodcuts. New Edition. Crown 8vo. 7s. 6d.

PRICE EIGHTEENPENCE, MONTHLY,

THE PRACTITIONER:
A Journal of Therapeutics and Public Health.

EDITED BY

T. LAUDER BRUNTON, M.D., F.R.S.,

*Fellow of the Royal College of Physicians;
Assistant Physician to St. Bartholomew's Hospital; and Lecturer on Materia Medica and Therapeutics in St. Bartholomew's Hospital School.*

CONTENTS.

Original Communications—Reviews of Books—Clinic of the Month—Extracts from British and Foreign Journals—Notes and Queries—Bibliography—and the Public Health Department.

In Quarterly Parts, price 3s. 6d.

BRAIN:
A JOURNAL OF NEUROLOGY.

EDITED BY

J. C. BUCKNILL, M.D., M.R.C.P., F.R.S.
J. CRICHTON-BROWNE, M.D., F.R.S.E.
D. FERRIER, M.D., F.R.C.P., F.R.S.
J. HUGHLINGS-JACKSON, M.D., F.R.C.P.

CONTENTS—Original Articles, consisting mainly of Clinical and Pathological Records and Anatomical and Physiological Researches, Human and Comparative, on the Nervous System. Signed Critical Digests and Reviews of Clinical, Experimental and other Researches in this department of Science, both at home and abroad. Foreign Correspondence. It will be the object of "BRAIN" to keep its readers well abreast of modern progress in Neurology, and to advance the knowledge of a class of disease respecting which it is universally admitted that much has yet to be learnt.

THE JOURNAL OF PHYSIOLOGY.

EDITED

(With the co-operation in England of Prof. A. GAMGEE, F.R.S., of Manchester; Prof. W. RUTHERFORD, F.R.S., of Edinburgh; Prof. J. B. SANDERSON, F.R.S., of London; and in America of Prof. H. P. BOWDITCH, of Boston; Prof. H. N. MARTIN, of Baltimore; and Prof. H. C. WOOD, of Philadelphia) by

DR. MICHAEL FOSTER, F.R.S.,

Of Trinity College, Cambridge.

It is proposed to publish it in parts, not at rigidly fixed times, but according to the supply of material. Every effort, however, will be made to prevent any unnecessary irregularity in the appearance of the successive parts. About four or six parts, the exact number depending on the size of the several parts, will form a volume of about 500 pages. The volume will not necessarily coincide with the year; its issue, like that of the constituent parts, will depend on the abundance of contributions.

The subscription-price for the volume, *post free*, will be, when paid in advance—

For Great Britain or America ... ... £1 1s., or $5.25 (gold).

Each part, as well as each volume, may also be obtained in the usual way through the trade, at the rate of £1 11s. 6d. per volume, the exact price of each part, being dependent on its size, &c.

www.ingramcontent.com/pod-product-compliance
Lightning Source LLC
Chambersburg PA
CBHW030406170426
43202CB00010B/1510